DECISION POINT

How the decisions you make, make you

Dieter Jansen

DECISION POINT

For Martine

Your decisions make this dad proud

CONTENTS

Acknowledgements 1

Foreword 3

Introduction.. 5

Setting the Scene: The Decision Point House....................9

Cracks in the Foundation... 15

Cracks in the Walls 16

Cracks in the Roof Tiles... 17

Major Alterations in Older Houses 17

It's My Perspective... 18

Your Perspective... 19

PART A: Frame of Reference — The External Influences

....**21**

What am I thinking? 23

Assumption: What is a "good" leader? 23

Ambiguity: How do I lead by example?.................... 26

Uncertainty: Where do I lead from?........................ 30

What do I believe? 37

Focus: What do I concentrate on? 37

Drivers: What beliefs determine my actions? 40

What am I experiencing?.. 46

Example: Who do I learn from? 46

Authority: How much does my opinion count? 49

Culture: Why is this the way we do things?............. 53

We are not clean slates.. 58
PART B: Decision Points — The Internal Choices...........61
Foundational Decision Points....................................**65**
Impact: Play to Win or Play not to Lose? 66
Respect: All or Only Some?................................ 71
Center: To Serve or to Be Served? 76
Priority: People First or Finance First?.................. 79
Perspective: Eternal or Earthly?.......................... 85
Character Decision Points......................................**95**
Contribution: Serving Down or Serving Up?................ 96
Model: Example or Excuse?.................................. 101
Teachability: Tell You or Teach Me?...................... 106
Authenticity: Open Book or Guarded Vault?............. 112
Freedom: Manipulate or Emancipate?................... 117
Ego: Conviction or Stubbornness? 126
Pressure: Popular or Principle?........................... 131
Criticism: Energizing or Discouraging? 136
Intentionality: Growth or Stagnation?................... 142
Source: Intuition or Information?......................... 146
Diligence: Wing It or Work at It? 156
Behavioral Decision Points.................................... **161**
Commitment: Promise or Possibility?.................... 162
Resilience: Diesel or Dynamite?........................... 167
Discipline: Public or Private?.............................. 176
Positioning: Part of the Team or Apart from the Team? . 184
Consistency: Dependable Vision or Random Messages? .. 190
Peacemaker: Competition or Collaboration?................ 197
Epilogue — The completed Decision Point House........ **203**
PART C: Build your own House **205**
Your Decision Point House................................208

• CONTENTS •

Instructions 214
What happens now? **223**
List of References **225**

ACKNOWLEDGEMENTS

This book took around 35 years to research, unbeknownst to me, with input from hundreds of sources. It's said that the student is never greater than the master, so I thank all those people with whom I have had interactions, positive or negative, who have contributed to this product.

Special thanks to those individuals who have allowed me to include their stories.

Thank you to my review panel: Eric Sparrow, Karl-Heinz Weber, Kate Ellis, Danielle Sparrow, Alexi Prodromou, Wessel Bentley, Kirk Anderson, Abraham Mosimi, Patrick Kleu and Dale Sparrow. Your valuable input has helped to make this a more robust product.

Elaine Broekman and Rachel-Mari Ackermann for the copy-editing, cover design and publication.

Ryno Kotze and the crowd at Shumani RSA for sponsoring the first print run.

Most importantly, to my Creator God, this has been Your project all along, and You'll send it where it needs to go.

Thank you!

FOREWORD

The opening paragraph of Dieter Jansen's book, *Decision Point*, instantly made me want to read on. This, in my humble opinion, is mostly a clue to the rest of the content and it generally turns out to be a great read. This one certainly was.

What makes this book authentic is Dieter's use of his own life and leadership examples which move away from the generally borrowed theory found in many so-called leadership books. Building on the point of authenticity, Dieter's focus on respecting and treating people right is truly refreshing and a lost "art" in our digital age of distant leadership. The deepest authenticity of *Decision Point* is the acknowledgment of God's daily involvement in the lives of humankind. Leadership is, after all, God's idea.

Much research and times of deep reflection must have taken place for this book to be written in final form. It is a "now" message for leaders at every level and it is an especially useful book in the hands of up-and-coming leaders who are hungry for mentoring. Emerging leaders, who are willing to follow the pioneers who have created a path for new minds to emulate and to learn from while adding their own discoveries in this new era, will find this leadership journey a memorable one. The practical aspect of *Decision Point* is that you get to rate your leadership approach and it is very effective and mostly accurate for each individual. Enjoy this smart and well thought-through application as much as I did.

I believe that *Decision Point* will be displayed among the titles of many other great books on leadership that have been written throughout the decades.

Angelique du Toit
AUTHOR | INSPIRATIONAL SPEAKER | PODCASTER | PANELIST | BLOGGER
VIRTUALLY ANYWHERE

INTRODUCTION

L ife is messy.
Messy situations can happen anytime, anywhere. It's that discussion with a co-worker who puts you in a conflict situation; an employee you may need to let go; unintended consequences of an action; being called into an office and put on the spot; a spouse who wants to leave; a child who reveals they have an addiction; a secret that someone told you that now compromises your position; or even just a reaction to a situation. No matter how well you've planned it out, how many books you've read, how many insurance policies you've bought, there will be a time, actually many times, when life becomes messy. The circumstances may be of your own doing, the doings of others, accidents or real "acts of God", but you will find yourself slap-bang in the middle of a mess. You have to nail your colors to the mast and make a decision. This is a *Decision Point!*

Messy times require sound leadership. You have to navigate through them. Your choices and decisions, beliefs and mindsets, and words and actions during these times will not only define who you become, but they will also reveal who you are to yourself and others. Sometimes you will be proud of how you have coped, and other times you will know that you have fallen short. Don't worry, that's how all leaders fare, even the ones we think always get everything right.

Do we really need another leadership book? Look around you to see what is happening right there within your inner circle. Everybody is a leader, even if only to lead themselves. Everybody's actions have an impact on others—positive or negative. Everybody makes decisions every day. This book talks less about leadership being about strategy and tactics, but rather focuses on character, values and motives. If you can lead yourself well, in time, you will naturally lead others. This is a book for anybody with a pulse.

> *"Everybody is a leader, even if only to lead themselves."*

We learn leadership from others from the day we are born. We learn it from parents, friends, teachers, TV, and a myriad of other sources. We learn it from both positive and negative sources, and if we are mindful about it, we can use all of that knowledge well. All too often the role models we are either blessed or cursed with, subconsciously determine our actions, and we morph into their mold, sometimes even while knowing that there must be a better way. We simply don't have an example of what that better way might be, because we have blindly accepted the role models that have been thrown our way.

That said, the point of this book is not what others have done. The question is: *What will you choose to do?* It's simply too late to wait until the mess hits us in the face to find out what we are made of. We would do better by intentionally seeking out that which we choose to be. I would have so appreciated it if my dad, a good dad by most standards, had taught me that early in life—that sense of being intentional, and therefore in control of my own development. I thought it would just happen, and developing a five-year plan was as foreign to me then as a cassette tape is to my daughter now. In retrospect, maybe he did try and tell me, but I wasn't listening...

Looking at my own development as a person and leader, there have been many decision points, beliefs and thoughts that challenged and shaped what I now believe a good leader to be. No doubt, there will be more. I was not the uber-leader in my younger years, at school and varsity and such, so I had a lot to learn. My own leadership bar was initially low, but through application, and eventually intention, my skills improved dramatically.

We are all familiar with the inspiring accounts of Gandhi, Mandela, Mother Teresa, various movie personalities and so forth. While important and invaluable for our inspiration, I have purposely not used these well-known nuggets of wisdom and put in some of my own. I did this for two reasons:

Firstly, authenticity. Much of this book will be about examining and criticizing internal issues of belief, character and behavior, and quite frankly, I have a tough enough job doing that with myself without pretending to be in a position to know other people well enough to do it.

Secondly, accessibility. If you are like me, then you will look at some of these well-known examples with a certain degree of awe and feel that they must have possessed something special to become who they did. I prefer you to think, "Well, if that guy can have some success, then so can I."

Finally, while these are my examples, that is *all* they are—examples. This book is not about me, it is about you. In writing this book, I hope to inspire you to learn more about yourself. I'm providing a framework based on certain decision points that have formed my leadership style, and if you follow with me, you will have the space to think through and build your own decision-point framework.

At the back of the book I have set up your own canvas for you to paint on. As we go through the stages, you will think through the questions and fill in your own framework.

Most importantly, I hope this book will inspire you to think how your leadership style impacts others, whether you lead yourself, your home, your family, a large organization, or all of the above. By making some small adjustments, your effectiveness as a leader will be dramatically improved, as well as the effectiveness of the future leaders... who are inspired by you.

SETTING THE SCENE: THE DECISION POINT HOUSE

"One of the dominant themes from our research is that breakthrough results come about by a series of good decisions, diligently executed and accumulated one on top of another."

— Jim Collins, *Good to Great.*[1]

T he cover of this book depicts a maze of decision points connected by pathways. Once we make a decision, we travel along a particular path, until we hit the next decision point, and so on. Decision points are interlinked, and the results of decisions we have made earlier will impact how we make the next decision.

However, not all decision points are created equal. Some are at a core level that defines why we even exist, others will reveal what we stand for, and still others are determined, in part, by the particular circumstances we find ourselves in. But all decisions do stack up eventually, and our foundational beliefs and character decision points will reveal themselves in our behavioral decisions, and how we show up in the world.

As a practical example, consider two dentists. Neither of them had been coerced into becoming a dentist by various pressures or the perception of making a lot of money. These two dentists both felt passionately that this was what they wanted to do and could not think of doing anything else. At this point we might assume they would be quite similar. A dedicated dentist is a dedicated dentist, right?

However, what if they had different views on life and where they could best serve in their profession? Supposing one had a heart for the elderly, and the other was drawn to working with actors and supermodels. The first would be involved in restoring dignity for people, the second would be enhancing individuals' careers. All subsequent decisions would flow from that. Would the dental practice be situated in an accessible area on the ground floor, or would it be in a trendy high rise? Would it be simple and functional, or would it be upmarket with a lounge? What kind of staff would they hire? How and what would they charge? And how would the dentist be dressed and groomed? These may sound like simple strategies to attract the right customers, but it's more than just that; it's an expression of who the dentists are! If we took those two dentists, completely fulfilled by what they do, and exchanged them—moved the Hollywood dentist to the Retirement Home dentist's practice and vice versa—in a short time both dentists would feel like they were wasting their time and not doing what they believed in. If left long enough, they would gradually, but inevitably migrate their practices to resemble their beliefs and convictions.

Like the two dentists, our inner world defines our decisions, and our decisions reveal us to the outer world. Therefore, our inner beliefs and convictions define who we ultimately become. It is wise to be awake and intentional when making the decisions that support, and add to, the beliefs we choose. These decisions have the potential of lasting a lifetime, or even longer, through the impact we have on others.

> *"Our inner world defines our decisions, and our decisions reveal us to the outer world."*

Looking back at the decisions that I've had to make in my life, I recognize that they can be placed on one of three levels, namely:

1. **Foundational** decision points are decisions that are at my very core; convictions and beliefs that I have chosen and that I effectively bet my life on. This is *why* I exist.

2. **Character** decision points are decisions that have shaped my values and ethics, and are strongly informed by the foundational beliefs. This is *what* I stand for.

3. **Behavioral** decision points are the decisions that have formed the basis of my leadership style and expression. They are in alignment with my foundational beliefs and character traits, but these decisions' outcomes could be dependent on current circumstances. This is *how* I show up.

However, our stories don't begin simply with the decisions we make. Before we become aware of even making decisions, our frame of reference, or environment, has shaped many of our thoughts and beliefs. We adopt these from our parents, our culture, and our day-to-day experiences. Before we can make truly informed decisions, we need to investigate which basic beliefs our environment has instilled within us, and decide whether they are valid and helpful, or flawed and ineffective.

It makes sense to me to show this in the form of a picture. Because I'm thinking of a "foundation" and an "environment", an image of a house seems to be a logical framework. For ease of use I've also given each environmental reference topic and each decision point a simple name that indicates what it is about. The whole picture is in the context of leadership, and the entire house would be the sum total of decision blocks, and therefore represents me.

The **"References"** section comprises the circumstances that have come my way over time that I have simply adopted. In the house framework these would be represented by the references that are considered when designing a house, such as landscape, style, other existing homes that serve as examples, building guidelines, prevailing weather patterns, etc. Those that are relevant are adopted, others are ignored, and some are specifically decided against. I've defined eight environmental topics (or references) for myself, namely: Ambiguity, Authority, Assumption, Example, Uncertainty, Culture, Drivers and Focus. We'll look at these in depth in Part A.

The **foundation** consists of my foundational decision points—the beliefs that I have adopted. In the framework these are the bricks that are below ground. How these blocks are put together determines the potential height, breadth and shape of the house. I've identified five foundational decision points, namely: Impact, Respect, Center, Priority and Perspective. They are explained in detail in Part B.

The **walls** are built with my character decision points. In the framework these are the bricks in the walls. They form the bulk of the outward appearance of the house, and determine whether the house is attractive, functional... or some other adjective. They define the character of the house. I've defined eleven such character decision points for myself, namely: Contribution, Model, Teachability, Authenticity, Freedom, Ego, Pressure, Criticism, Intentionality, Source and Diligence. They are also explained in detail in Part B.

The **roof** is laid out with my behavioral decision points. In the framework these are the roof tiles, and they can be replaced and interchanged without severely impacting the rest of the house. I've defined six behavioral decision points for myself, namely: Commitment, Resilience, Discipline, Positioning, Consistency and Peacemaker. They are explained in detail in Part B.

The house is built over time, and as decision points are reached, certain flaws may be revealed. Reference factors may also change, which require a revamp of some of the house's aspects. And, of course, there is the never-ending task of maintenance, to ensure that the house stands strong. We may even consider some major renovations

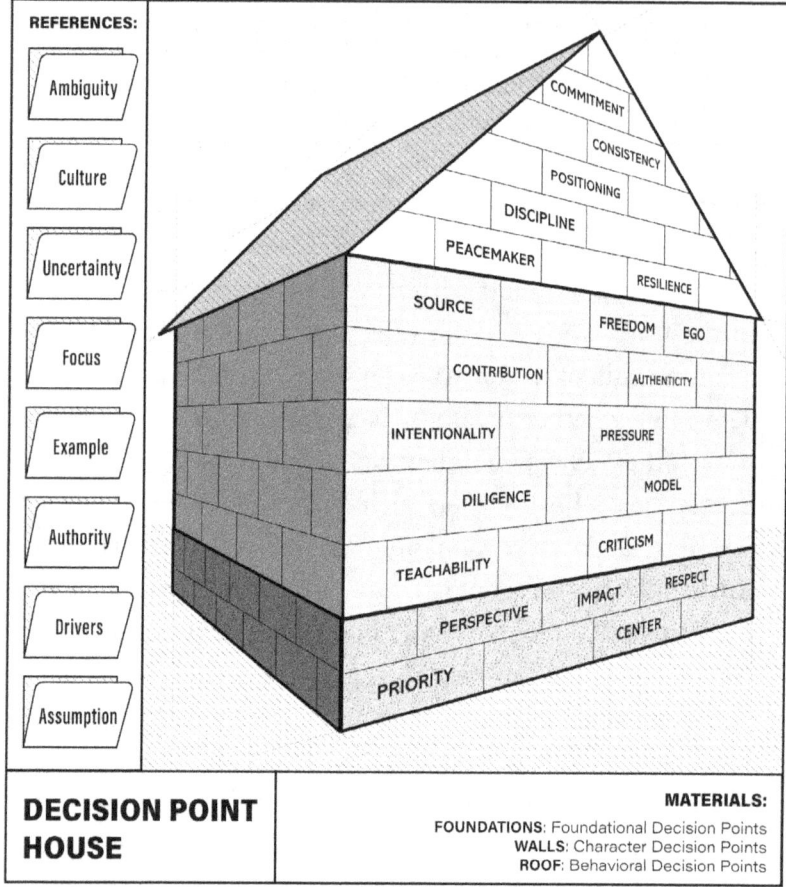

DECISION POINT HOUSE

REFERENCES:
- Ambiguity
- Culture
- Uncertainty
- Focus
- Example
- Authority
- Drivers
- Assumption

MATERIALS:
FOUNDATIONS: Foundational Decision Points
WALLS: Character Decision Points
ROOF: Behavioral Decision Points

over time as the events in our lives unfold. Just like a physical house, it is always a work in progress in some form.

Cracks in the Foundation

The foundational decision points will impact all other decision points. Cracks in the foundation will propagate up into the walls and even the roof. Decisions will not be robust or consistent, and the house that has been built could be in danger of toppling if left long enough. At best, it will limit what the house is capable of achieving.

If you make a decision that is in conflict with your foundational belief, you will feel it. It will not be long before a cognitive dissonance arises that will urge you to make a change. In practical terms, this could be a situation at work where you have to take an action that goes against a core belief. You might even have witnessed some injustice happening and doing something about it would be costly, but keeping quiet becomes extremely uncomfortable.

> *"If you make a decision which is in conflict with your foundational belief, you will feel it."*

Another possibility is that you are not yet aware of having to make a certain foundational decision. For example, if you have not set any goals in life, you can work in any job that seems appropriate. In the house analogy, you may be building a house, walls and all, only to discover later that it isn't the design you want, and you have to start over, or settle for what you have.

On the other hand, you may avoid making a foundational decision because it is inconvenient, or painful. The crack in the foundation is plastered closed with justifications and blind eyes, but the effects are felt in character issues and day-to-day decisions. This may be an addiction of some sort that you are unwilling to face, or a known false belief that you choose to hang on to because it has some advantage. In both these cases you are dishonest with yourself.

Cracks and foundations don't do well together, and the sooner these are opened up and properly dealt with, the sooner your house will be able to carry the load for which it has been designed.

Cracks in the Walls

Character decision points determine how the people whom we interact with see us. If you have a crack in the character part of your house, your behavioral decision points will be impacted. Other people will be affected, and this could change your future interactions. At the same time, the character crack could be a pointer to a crack in your foundation, so it must be investigated. However, if it is only a character crack, it can be fixed and restored with some care and work.

For example, you may have a habit of being overly critical, or not taking advice, or always justifying your own actions. These are annoying to your followers, could impact the trust relationship you have with others and make you less effective as a leader. However, the house, the person, is still inherently safe. Your ability to weather challenges may be compromised in the long run, though.

Cracks in the Roof Tiles

Our behaviors will be a direct result of our character decision points, and even our foundational decision points. Within those boundaries, however, we have a certain degree of flexibility, and circumstances will determine the decisions to be made. If we make a behavioral decision that is in conflict with our character, we may feel uncomfortable for a while, but we can move on. Generally, there is no massive harm done, and things can be rectified quite easily.

With regards to the behavioral decision points there is no single correct way of doing things. The same person can be faced with similar decision points but decide differently for a variety of reasons. This does not impact the integrity of the character decision points and will always be open to debate and criticism.

In the house analogy, if there is a crack in a roof tile, then replace the tile, and move on. If you want to change the color of the entire roof, you can do so without influencing the integrity of the house. The roof is still a necessary part of the house, though. It also helps to weather life's storms.

Major Alterations in Older Houses

In our minds we tend to think that our houses are rock-solid and fixed, providing a place of peace and safety. If we are an "older" house, we could wrongly believe that we can't change things anymore. After all, the saying goes that you can't teach an old dog new tricks. This is simply not true. The truth is that doing something new requires change, and our learned comfort is what keeps us from making changes. We typically also have more to lose if we are going to make a substantial change later in life. However, it still remains a choice that we have full control over, and if we have the desire to do something new or make big changes, it is well within our reach to do so.

It's My Perspective

My house is made up of the decision points that I have been faced with, affected by or been party to at least once over the years. I believe everyone goes through a similar set of decisions, although your set of decisions may look different. You may even classify them differently. This book describes my perspective, and as such, my bias towards a certain course of action will probably show. That doesn't mean it is correct, it just means it's my perspective.

Whichever way you choose to categorize your decision points, remember that the foundational ones will have the most impact on your life and determine how you approach the other decisions. They are also potentially the most elusive, because whether you're aware of them or not, you have certain beliefs. These could serve you... or work against you. I would urge you to spend time with a program or coach to investigate these beliefs, and either solidify them if they are valid or replace them if they are unhelpful.

Your Perspective

Your perspective may be completely different to mine. You may find some of my foundational decision points are your character decision points and so on. You may also find some of my decision points are not at all valid in your circumstances. You most likely will also find some additional decision points that I haven't identified.

After every section in the book, there are a few questions with spaces for answers. I would strongly encourage you not to answer the questions with the first thoughts that pop up in your mind, but to first take five minutes to *think* about what you are thinking about. In this way you will get the most value out of your time investment. Finally, a summary table and a blank "Decision Point House" framework is included in Part C of this book. Transferring your answers into these will give you a more complete picture of how you make decisions, and how your house is defined.

Ultimately, it's your perspective that will mean the most to you, and having thought about it and then built your "Decision Point House", I'll guarantee that you will begin to notice and recognize how your decision points show up in your life and in your leadership journey.

PART A:
FRAME OF REFERENCE —
THE EXTERNAL INFLUENCES

B y the time we wake up to the idea of actually leading ourselves and others, we have already had many years of circumstantial and environmental conditioning. To a large extent, ironically, that conditioning determined how soon we woke up to the idea in the first place... or whether we woke up at all.

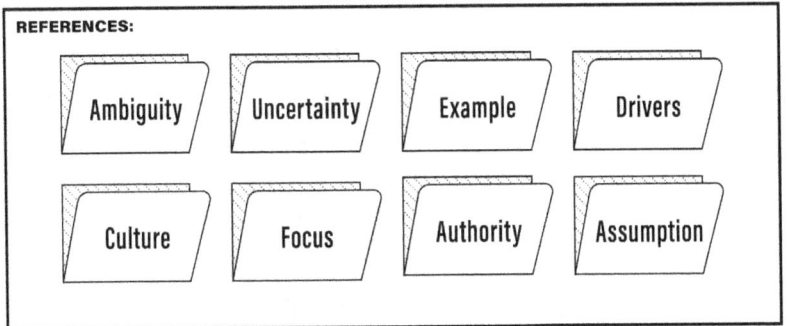

We are not clean slates. Every book, every idea and every statement will be filtered through our frame of reference, or paradigm, and influence our response. We may think we are making objective decisions, but we are not objective. We can't be, because we only have our point of view.

Our point of view, which has evolved from our experiences, perceptions, prejudices, and years of influence from outside sources, mostly was not of our own choosing. Whether I believe this way or that way is often simply a product of what I was led to believe.

This reminds me of a time when I was very young and my brother, five years my senior, explained that farmers feed their cows milk powder, get them to drink water and run around in the pasture for a while. In the evening the cows would then present the farmer with the milk that they have "mixed" during the day. I thought my brother was one of the smartest people I knew. He must have thought the opposite about me, because I carried that theory with me for quite a while until one day, when I decided to investigate it a little... Hang on a second!

Cows and farmers aside, many of the ideas that are planted in our minds as young kids establish our way of thinking and our beliefs. Potentially, for life. Often, these ideas and beliefs are buried so deep that we don't even know we have them. They also don't show up the same for everybody.

So, just because my brother and I grew up in the same home, doesn't necessarily mean our beliefs will be exactly the same. Similar maybe, but still different.

In our quest to become better and more effective individuals and leaders, we must interrogate our own paradigms to see how they build us up, trip us up, or blow us up.

We have to step outside of ourselves and continually ask ourselves these three questions:

- What am I thinking?
- What do I believe?
- What am I experiencing?

> *"We must interrogate our own paradigms to see how they build us up, trip us up, or blow us up."*

The more we ask ourselves these questions and experiment with the answers, the more we bring subconscious thought patterns to the fore, and the more we can strip out the defective ones.

What am I thinking?

Assumption: What is a "good" leader?

In almost every leadership training program I have taught, a discussion erupted around the definition of a "good" leader. It usually started like this: "Hitler must have been a good leader because he managed to mobilize millions of people towards a common objective."

And then the debate would start.

This is a legitimate question. What exactly defines a "good" leader? John C Maxwell[7], international leadership expert and profound influencer in my life, asserts that *"Leadership is influence. Nothing more, nothing less."* However, if we are to go about defining leadership purely by that standard on face value then Hitler, and many others, could be regarded as "good" leaders. They undoubtedly had enormous influence. Although, if you are familiar with Maxwell's work, you will know that he has a heart for people, and his definition of a good leader would not only include the level of influence someone has, but also the quality of that influence, the motivation behind that influence, and the follower's freedom to choose.

So, the question of a good leader is actually two questions. Firstly, is the leader good, as opposed to evil? This is a *character* question, encompassing ethics, values, awareness and self-image. Secondly, is the leader good, as opposed to weak? This is a *competence* question, encompassing skill, behaviors, talent and strategy.

Going back to the Hitler debate, my usual response has been to allow the debate to go on a little, and then to ask two questions to reach a conclusion. The first was, "How did Hitler gain power?" The answers here usually ranged from clever tactics, strategy and conniving, to instilling fear, ruthless removal of naysayers and paranoia. The second question was, "Would you like to work for Hitler, trusting him with your career?" I have yet to encounter someone who answers with an unreserved, "Yes!" While we may be able to learn a thing or two from Hitler's competence as a leader, it would always be colored by his beliefs and character, and most of us would not trust those.

Personally, I would like to add another question which I think should precede the first two. "What does the leader believe?" This is a foundational question and interrogates the leader's motivation, purpose, morals and tenacity.

Therefore, for the purposes of this book, the generic term "good leader" applies to all three. Belief, character and competence are all indistinguishable from the leader, and decisions the leader makes will inevitably be influenced by these aspects. In the following chapters we will take a closer look at each of these aspects as well as some key decisions that ultimately form the leader. But first, in this chapter I would like to lay the groundwork in understanding how our thoughts, beliefs, and character are influenced and ultimately formed, often by the leaders and role models in our lives. It is important to understand this in order to make better-informed decisions, which are outlined in the later chapters.

I recently read a book which attempted to move away from "personality-driven" leadership, and rather put processes and structures in place that would outlive the leader and carry on long after he or she has left the building. While I agree with the sentiment and aim of the author, I'm not sure that it is always achievable. If a leader's impact is influenced by his beliefs, character and competence, then the leader's best chance at sustaining what has been achieved is to have strong succession plans with people who have the same beliefs, similar character traits and level of competence. However, if the leader is not in control of his successor, then the new leader will undoubtedly shape the environment according to their own beliefs and character, which may not be the same. The new leader can only lead from their own core. They cannot do otherwise.

Then there is the question of timing. I believe that circumstances suit different leaders at different periods in time, such as the example of Churchill who had been lauded as a great war-time prime minister, and then ousted in the elections once the war was over. Leaders aren't all good at leading people in all situations; they each have specific niches. For anyone who wishes to be a good and effective leader, it's crucial to know in which types of circumstances and environments they can lead well, and equally important, to know which to stay away from.

All of the above is simply to say that the answer to "What makes a leader good?" is subjective, even if all their belief and character issues are acceptable to us. No two leaders will operate exactly the same way. Based on our formative events, we make decisions daily, on autopilot, without thinking. Going back to the Hitler debate, if you were asked whether you would like to work for Hitler, your answer would already give a pointer to the type of leader that you want to be. Your answer would be influenced by your foundational beliefs and the character you aspire to. And so, step by step, decision points will pop up in your life to form the leader you will ultimately be.

Ambiguity: How do I lead by example?

I have had a varied career, to say the least. In addition to various roles in two companies, I also found myself in a variety of industries as a result of our varied client base.

My roles often required me to facilitate workshops about leadership in one form or another. Here "leader" is a very broad definition, and not limited to a position. When asked what kind of leadership people wanted, one answer always came up: "Leading by example." But when I asked what "leading by example" actually meant to them, their answers were very diverse. In some cases, people are looking for a leader that knows how to do everything *they* can do—only better. You may have come across this expectation by being asked, or by saying, something along these lines: "You've never soldered anything in your life. How are you going to teach me anything?" This was an actual event. In this case, "example" means a technical master.

In another case where I wanted an appointment with an academic leader, I was told that they had several people with PhD's in various subjects reporting to them, and therefore I probably couldn't have anything to add? In this case, "example" meant a superior and greater level of knowledge.

Lastly, in my favorite case, when I was promoted to foundry manager, I was pledged support by a rough and ready maintenance manager, many years my senior, with the words, "I don't believe you are enough of a bastard to succeed at this job, but while you are here, I will support you." In this case, "example" meant a particular leadership style. This is my favorite example, by the way, because two years later the same maintenance manager applauded my team on having achieved better results than we had ever achieved before, and by all accounts I had not turned into a "bastard".

There are many other possibilities, for example, the best ideas, the best strategies, the best opportunities, but they all fall short when there is an expectation that the leader is the best at everything. The final nail in this particular coffin comes when good leaders say that they aim to surround themselves with individuals who are better than they are. So how would *they* lead by example?

People simply don't know how to articulate what they are looking for in a leader who "leads by example". The knowledge view doesn't work, because the CEO of a research institute cannot possibly know more than all his employees. The technical master view falls flat because a sports team's coach cannot play better than every player on the team. The leadership style expectation is also doomed because not everybody on the team would want the same type of leader. Yet, everybody wants someone that can set an example.

> *"It is not always necessary to have the technical knowledge in order to add value to the team."*

What people are asking for when they would like someone to lead by example, is actually a leader they can trust, respect, and learn from in a positive sense. A leader who will put themselves on the line for the team, value the team members, and help them achieve their goals, as well as the organization's goals. A leader with a vision and an ability to achieve results with and through the team. In short, they are looking for a *positive* role model.

This is good news for leaders who are focused on the team's development. It is not always necessary to have the technical knowledge in order to add value to the team. By way of example, a few years ago, I was an executive coach to Ryno Kotze, the MD of Shumani RSA, a printing company running 24-hour production, five days a week. Ryno then employed me on a part-time basis to improve production. Officially, I was the head of production. I had production experience and people skills, but when it came to printing, I wasn't even competent to change the cartridge on my home printer. I had absolutely no clue about this industry, and my appointment must have come as a shock to many of the team members. But Ryno sold it well, and I put my best efforts into getting to know the team members and some of the intricacies of the processes. What I discovered, not surprisingly, was that the supervisors and team leaders really knew their stuff, and really didn't need my advice on any printing issues. In fact, as a coach, I knew to ask them the relevant questions and then they would figure things out themselves. They were a great group of individuals, but they needed to be turned into a great team. We made a number of operational changes, and then developed a strong vision for the one hundred or so production people to focus on. We also implemented weekly meetings where I would meet with the employees of every shift for 10 minutes. These meetings were held at 6am, 2pm and 10pm every week and gave me the opportunity to direct the vision and train the greater team. We called this a "drip-feed" approach. In addition, we developed production measures that told the team how we were doing. We put all this in place fairly quickly, and despite early setbacks, just kept at it, waiting for the law of cause and effect to run its course (see "Focus" in the next section). The theory was finally proven when, in November that year—traditionally the busiest month— sales and production were the highest the company had ever achieved, and it was achieved with uncharacteristically low wastage and the lowest overtime cost to date.

The purpose of this example is to illustrate that skill in leadership is universally applicable and can add value across industries and in different-sized companies. As a good leader, you can lead by example anywhere, and be a positive role model to many individuals.

Uncertainty: Where do I lead from?

When we watch movies and read books, we are often inspired by the stories of larger-than-life leaders, boldly leading the charge, and charismatically getting followers to commit to a cause. But what does that say about many of us who aren't that extroverted, nor good at inspiring speeches, nor ever out in front? Does that mean we aren't meant to be leaders? The mistake we are making is to compare ourselves, often prior to gaining any leadership experience,

> "Our greatest challenge comes from leading ourselves."

with some of the great leaders in history. Of course, we will fall short! In fact, those great leaders would also have fallen short at the beginning of their leadership journeys. It's a process.

When presenting leadership training, there are often individuals who question whether they should even be there, because they don't officially lead anyone. But that isn't true. Our greatest challenge comes from leading ourselves. We can easily advise someone else on what they should do, but it's far more difficult for us to do what we know we should be doing. Leading ourselves well is the basis for our foundational decision points. This is good news, because you can start today, no matter where you find yourself. If you lead yourself well, in time, you will naturally lead others.

If you still need convincing, then ask yourself these simple questions:

- Do you speak, or communicate, at any time during the day?
- When you speak, is somebody listening?
- Does what you say influence what they think, do or say?

The answers to these are mostly yes for everybody for at least a single moment a day, so that puts you in a position of leadership in that moment. If at any time you are asked to show someone something, or explain something, or give an opinion, that is a leadership moment. Those moments place a responsibility on you to lead well, even if they are seemingly insignificant.

Additionally, if you have children, you are leading. Period.

It is an interesting debate where leaders should lead from, and in what situations. Here are four situations that highlight varying positions from which leaders lead:

EXAMPLE 1: LEADING FROM THE FRONT

The movie, *Glory*[2], is based on the true story of the 54th Regiment of Massachusetts, the first black regiment to fight for the North in the American Civil war. Its commander, a young Colonel Robert Shaw, played by Matthew Broderick, trained and led these men. Shaw led from the front. When his regiment didn't receive the uniforms and boots that were required, he led a small band to "acquire" what was needed from the quarter-master. When the 54th voluntarily led the charge to take Fort Wagner, by all accounts a suicide mission, Shaw was right in front. More than half of his men lost their lives in the battle, and Shaw himself was also killed. Although short-lived, he was undeniably an inspiration to his men.

EXAMPLE 2: LEADING FROM THE BACK

Another war-time mini-series[3], *Band of Brothers*, is a true story that follows the men of Easy Company, of the 101st Airborne division, from their training just prior to the invasion of Normandy to the end of World War II. One of the conscripts who developed into an excellent leader was Lieutenant Dick Winters. Winters, like Shaw, led from the front, jumping up out of ditches under fire to get his men to move forward, always leading the attack. Some didn't know how he managed to survive. Later, he was promoted to battalion commander, and in the battle to take the town of Foy, Easy Company got into trouble because their new leader was indecisive. Captain Winters's instinct was to run into the fray and help out, but his commanding officer prohibited him from doing so, expecting him to direct the battle from a safer distance. Winters sent in another leader who managed to successfully continue the attack.

EXAMPLE 3: LEADING FROM THE MIDDLE

In their excellent book[4], *Extreme Ownership*, former US Navy SEALs, Jocko Willink and Leif Babin, highlight the importance of where officers are positioned during SEAL training. If they are too far forward in the operation, they get sucked into the minute details of their specific area and cannot see the big picture. If they are too far to the back, they lose sight of what is going on in the frontlines and become disconnected from the team. According to them, an officer's position should be somewhere in the middle where they would have the best understanding of the entire situation, free to move to wherever they are needed to direct operations.

EXAMPLE 4: LEADING FROM BEHIND THE SCENES

While an effective leader will never truly simply be behind the scenes, this leading style has more to do with the motivation of the leader and their reluctance to take personal credit for any successes. In his book[1], *Good to Great*, Jim Collins describes his research project where 1,435 Fortune 500 companies were analyzed to find which had become "great" companies. The criteria for "great company" were that the company had gone through a transition point, followed by a period of at least 15 years of significantly outperforming the stock market. Of the 1,435 companies, only 11 made the grade, outperforming the stock market by between 342% and 1,850%. The research goes into a number of factors that these eleven companies had in common. One of the surprising common factors was the type of leadership each company had at the time of the transition. These leaders were typically strong-willed, stoic and committed to the company success, while at the same time modest, self-effacing and understated. Collins terms this "Level 5" leadership and says the following:

> "Given that Level 5 leadership cuts against the grain of conventional wisdom, especially the belief that we need larger-than-life saviors with big personalities to transform companies, it is important to note that Level 5 is an empirical finding, not an ideological one."

In other words, this is not merely theory, it was proven by extensively researching real case studies. How do we recognize who these "Level 5" leaders are, since they aren't accompanied by lots of fanfare? Collins's advice is this:

> "Look for situations where extraordinary results exist but where no individual steps forth to claim excess credit. You will likely find a potential Level 5 leader at work."

These examples are not mutually exclusive, meaning that the same leader may lead from different positions, depending on the specific situation. They may also seem simplistic, mixing military and organizational examples.

However, the examples show that there is not just one way to lead, and hopefully they will break down some misconceptions of what leaders have to be like.

The fact is that, regardless of where you find yourself, you can develop your own leadership style, and in each unique situation you will have to decide where to properly position yourself, and what will motivate your leadership decisions.

YOUR TURN

1. What kind of leader do you want to be?

   _____

   _____

   _____

   _____

2. How would you lead by example?

   _____

   _____

   _____

3. Where would you be best suited to lead from?

   _____

   _____

   _____

ADDITIONAL THOUGHTS

_____

_____

_____

_____

_____

_____

_____

_____

_____

_____

_____

_____

_____

_____

_____

What do I believe?

Focus: *What do I concentrate on?*

The law of cause and effect is important to note in our leadership development because it keeps us from putting the cart before the horse. We don't get (official) leadership opportunities and then learn how to lead. We will mostly get leadership opportunities *because* we have displayed some leadership qualities. Those leadership qualities have been developed within us, possibly before we even knew we were in the running to become leaders. We more than likely displayed our leadership qualities by how we led ourselves.

A tried-and-tested example of cause and effect is the planting of seeds and harvesting of crops. We bury seeds in the ground, and diligently water the seeds, even when we see no progress. Some days or weeks go by, and eventually we see some shoots pushing through the ground surface. We continue to water and feed the plants. They continue to grow… and eventually the crop is ready. We harvest the crop and reap the rewards. Using this analogy, I want to draw out a few obvious points:

1. If we don't plant, we won't reap a harvest. We have to invest in doing the work that the process requires in order to achieve the reward at the end.

2. If we don't have faith in the process, we will give up. We water seeds even though we don't initially see any progress. We have faith that the underground work is being done and that the harvest will come, as long as we do the necessary work for as long as it is required.

3. If we try to harvest before the crop is ripe, we ruin the reward. We cannot force things to develop faster than they naturally will. We can set up an environment that is most conducive to growth, but the growth happens at its own pace.

Now let's go deeper. James Allen[5] wrote *As a man thinketh* over a hundred years ago. When Allen refers here to "thought", he refers to both rational thought and subconscious thought, namely belief.

Allen writes this:

> *"As the plant springs from, and could not be without, the seed, so every act of man springs from the hidden acts of thought, and could not have appeared without them. This applies equally to those acts called 'spontaneous' and 'unpremeditated' as to those which are deliberately executed."*

> *"Man is a growth by law, and not a creation by artifice, and cause and effect is as absolute and undeviating in the hidden realm of thought as in the world of visible and material things."*

This means that the same laws that govern a seed's growth into the plant it was designed to be, govern our thought life that develops us into the leaders that we become. This refers to both our conscious thoughts and subconscious beliefs, which will determine our actions. If we look at the three points above, all three of them hold true for our own leadership development:

1. In order to become the kind of leaders that we have the potential of becoming, we must intentionally invest in the process of growth. Success in leadership does not happen by chance.

2. Growth in leadership takes time and seems to have a time lag to it. We can easily give up when we have put in the time but don't perceive any results. We must continue to invest in the process, even when we don't see any outward changes, because as sure as the sun rises every morning, some internal subconscious work is being done to equip us for challenges that still lie ahead.

3. We can easily become impatient and try to move things along too quickly. We want the reward, but our investment hasn't prepared us well enough yet. We may prematurely ask for a position and set ourselves up for failure. Or we may simply decide that it's too much effort and settle for whatever comes our way.

Unlike the seeds in the analogy, which cannot decide which fruit to bear, we do have choices around our own leadership destiny. We can choose what kind of leader we want to be. We can choose what we want to reap as rewards. We can even choose what we wish to believe.

James Allen tells us that by becoming self-aware, and conscious of what we are thinking and doing, and why, we gain the possibility of making changes that will change our outcome. In fact, unless we change the way we think and what we believe, it is impossible to make any shifts in our leadership journey. Even if we go through life unaware of this developmental law, any shifts that we do make will be via the random influence of a person or environment that shifts our beliefs.

> "Stop focusing on the result and start focusing on the actions that cause the desired result."

Wouldn't it then make that much more sense to use this God-created process to our advantage and become intentional about our thoughts?

We mostly concentrate on the effects—the monthly report, the acknowledgement, or the title. Instead, we should focus on the actions that influence the monthly report, the acknowledgement, or the title, even if that result is in the distant future.

Stop focusing on the result and start focusing on the actions that cause the desired result. In good time, the appropriate results will come about.

Drivers: What beliefs determine my actions?

Maxwell Maltz had a successful career as a plastic surgeon. During that time, he found it curious that some patients would undergo massive psychological transformation as a result of plastic surgery, while in others the surgery would correct the physical, and yet the psychological remained the same. He came to understand the power of self-image in the healing process, and admitted that he often treated his patients successfully through discussion, thereby avoiding plastic surgery altogether.

In 1960 Maltz published his well-known book[6], *The New Psycho-Cybernetics*, which has sold over 30 million copies. He was 61 years old at the time. He summarizes the main concept of his book in one sentence:

*"Human beings will **always** act and feel and perform in accordance with what they **imagine** to be **true** about themselves and their environment."*

To put this into a practical example, imagine a place in the African Savannah. The grasslands interspersed with some thorn trees, a vibrant orange sunset, the far-off lazy roar of the king, followed by the high-pitched laughter of zebras. If you are from Africa, you would call this "the bush". If you are someone who enjoys the bush, you will be sitting in the grass with your favorite drink in hand, listening to the crackle of the fire for the *braai* (South African for barbeque). You would be completely at ease and at peace as the week's stress melts away. However, if you are someone who dislikes the bush, you would be cowering inside the cabin, anxious, heart palpitating, not daring to set a foot outside for fear of the beasts that could pounce on you and devour you. One person can experience complete peace, the other, sheer panic. It's important to note that for both people *the circumstances are identical!* The only difference is what they *imagine* to be *true* about their environment. The difference between peace and panic is choosing what to believe. Once believed, all conscious and subconscious actions flow from that. That is the power of belief.

There isn't a person alive without any beliefs. Some people actively question what they believe, and test to see if those beliefs are valid. However, most people carry on with the beliefs they have, often unaware of their existence. We can choose what to believe, and if we are to reach our potential, we have to diligently perform that belief interrogation. Only by changing flawed beliefs will we change long-term behavior.

> *"The difference between peace and panic is choosing what to believe."*

Here is an example of how subconscious beliefs can drive leadership behavior. I've been brought up to finish what I have started. At the same time, one of my subconscious driving forces in life has always been to be independent and at least have the perception of control over my own life. I don't know where this came from, but it's there, and plays out in all areas of my life. For example, I loved the freedom of back-packing through Europe and being able to hop on a train at any time and end up somewhere else if I wanted to. It also plays out in my leadership life. Early on in my career I was put in charge of a small new section (consisting of myself and one other person) which did computer simulations of metal-casting processes. While I had some experience in the field, my colleague, Adrian, had none. He was a metallurgist and understood solidification, but the computer simulation angle was new to him. I handed Adrian the software training manuals and asked him to go through them, promising that I would be available to answer any questions. It wasn't long before he returned to my office, threw the files on my desk and said, "I don't have a clue what's going on in here. You must explain it to me."

I got irritated and said, "Not like that. Once you've gone through the information and formed some type of opinion on how things work, even if it's wrong, we will have the basis for a conversation." Adrian, much annoyed, dutifully went off and went through the manuals. He went on to become an extremely gifted solidification simulation consultant, oftentimes showing me how to do certain things when I had run out of options. When I left the company a couple of years later, he reminded me of this conversation and said to me, "I was really peeved that day, but it turned out to be the most empowering thing you could have done. It forced me to think and figure it out for myself."

Now this is a great story, but don't think for a minute I was a "gifted leader" working for the best interests of my team at that point. The truth is that my subconscious need to remain independent and able to move on at a moment's notice was driving my reaction—and it was purely a reaction. I *needed* Adrian to be able to figure it out for himself. I *needed* him not to be dependent on me. I *needed* all of this so that I could satisfy my own two driving forces—finishing what I had started, as well as remaining independent and potentially mobile. Thus, my entire working career has been shaped by me getting people to figure things out on their own and developing them into people who could replace me... and then some. I became good at working myself out of a job so that I could move on to something new. I say this with humility. It was just simple, dumb luck that this *need* on my part turned out to be a very powerful leadership trait. Over time I began to truly appreciate the people I was developing, and only then could I claim that I was consciously leading.

The point that Maltz makes is clear, though. What we believe will impact how we act and, ultimately, the circumstances we will find ourselves in. Our beliefs impact all areas of our lives. It is said that how we do *something* is how we do *everything*. The driving force behind my leadership style was also the driving force behind how I raised my daughter. It's also the driving force behind my interactions with my running club and my running schedule.

How we do something is how we do everything. The good news is that the law of cause and effect implies that by changing the right thing (belief), we change everything.

YOUR TURN

1. What would focusing on the process instead of the result mean for you?

_____

_____

_____

_____

_____

_____

2. What core needs and desires drive your behavior?

_____

_____

_____

_____

_____

ADDITIONAL THOUGHTS

_____

_____

_____

_____

_____

_____

_____

_____

_____

_____

_____

_____

_____

_____

What am I experiencing?

Example: Who do I learn from?

I love inspirational movies, specifically those true stories of people who achieved much against all odds, either for themselves or for others. Ordinary people achieving extraordinary things. Some examples which immediately spring to mind are *Rudi, Remember the Titans,* and *The Freedom Writers.* There are many more. At the core of these movies are role models. These people are the reason I love the movies—they act as role models to me.

Role models represent a tangible, visual reminder of what we want to be like. They expand our minds to believe beyond what we currently see within ourselves. They give us a belief in something that we can achieve or aspire to become. This is, of course, if we have *positive* role models.

Negative role models will influence us in the opposite way. They are reminders of what we don't want to be like. They shrink our minds to believe less about ourselves and our environment. They also give us beliefs about what we cannot achieve, or never will become.

Whether positive or negative, role models *will* shape us. Especially when we are young, authority figures will impress on us beliefs that could potentially stay with us for the rest of our lives. These beliefs may subconsciously influence our behaviors and actions and mold the world we live in. When I coach executives, one of the key areas which I investigate is the "mantras" with which they grew up. These are the typical sayings that parents had often uttered that might have made an impact on a young mind.

I say *might* have made an impact, because they don't always stick. Two brothers growing up with the same mantra could respond with the one's life being governed by it, while the other brother may not even remember it. As an example, "If you're going to do something, do it properly!" sounds like good advice, but could also lead to indecision in leaders if the "proper" ways aren't clear. A teacher saying "You'll never amount to anything" could cause someone to subconsciously resist success in order to fit in with this picture. These parents and teachers aren't evil, but this is mentioned to simply serve as a reminder that a careless comment from someone in authority can make a lasting impact on a formative mind. If this comment is repeated over and over, it spells trouble. Likewise, if the comments are sincere, positive and uplifting, they could lay the foundation for future success.

But these are just the words. Actions by people in authority have an even greater impact. In John Maxwell's book, *21 Irrefutable Laws of Leadership*, the "Law of the Picture" is discussed. It basically states that *people do what people see*. We know this is true of our children. You can talk, teach, and coax the right things *ad infinitum*, but if your actions don't match up with the words, the kids will unfortunately do what you *do*, and not what you *say*. The same is true of our role models. We end up doing what they do. That is why, in the discussion of the "Law of the Picture", it is said that the most valuable gift a leader can give is being a good example.

The power that role models have in shaping our beliefs cannot be overstated. These newly-shaped beliefs then impact our behavior and our actions.

I'm reminded of a friend who was in a junior position in a company where the boss was autocratic and micromanaging. The boss was a great person outside of work, did a lot for her people, and had built a successful company. Yet her leadership style was quite daunting. My friend was well-versed with leadership books, read various articles, and knew how frustrated she felt in her position. Yet, when promoted to a leadership role, her leadership style exactly reflected her own boss's. Whether it was for survival I'm not sure, but the fact that she did not have an alternative example meant that she would default to the example she had. Such is the power of role models—we may even act contrary to how we think we will.

> *"The power that role models have in shaping our beliefs cannot be overstated."*

The good news is that once you become intentional about your leadership development, and understand the laws and processes that govern that development, you will also have the awareness and opportunity to make some choices. You can absolutely choose role models for yourself. Whether they be specific authors, TED-talk speakers, leader biographies, or mentors you seek out and speak with, you have the power to shape your own leadership concept. If your boss is not a good leader, you can use that information to shape your own leadership style, and when the time is right, move. If you perceive your boss as a good leader, ask them if they would be prepared to mentor you. Then, as you get the hang of it, you will see that you will need different mentors for different aspects of your desired leadership outcome.

Never forget that even while you are busy developing yourself by choosing role models, you are inevitably a role model to others. Your actions and your words matter, and in this you have an additional, powerful leadership development opportunity—being evaluated as a role model. Many of my insights have come from people whom I had led and who have subsequently commented on my leadership style, characteristics and failings.

Authority: How much does my opinion count?

The power that leaders have by virtue of their title and place in an organization's hierarchy is termed "positional power". Many authors and case studies, and even our own experiences, prove to us that having the position does not make you a good leader. It is still up to the leaders in question to develop themselves further to become good.

However, we cannot ignore the simple fact that the position does give the leader a certain degree of power and influence, and, in general, a good leader *with* the position is way more effective than a good leader without the position. In fact, a good leader without the position is often frustrated and hemmed in by the bad leader with the position. The leader in the position carries a huge amount of influence, and therefore can absolutely influence your leadership development. The positional leader is, after all, still an authority figure, and has an effect on your thinking and your decisions. Depending on the culture you live in, that effect can be small, or it could be potentially life-threatening.

In his book, *Outliers*, Malcolm Gladwell[8] investigates the causes of various aircraft crashes and makes the case that the deference to someone with positional power in certain cultures is partly responsible for these disasters. The deference of a Korean co-pilot, not willing to clearly point out mistakes by the senior pilot, may have contributed to the crash of Korean Air flight 801 in 1997, killing 223 people. Furthermore, 73 people lost their lives in 1990 when Avianca flight 52 ran out of fuel over New York, and crashed. Gladwell explains that the Colombian pilots were not assertive enough in explaining to the New York air traffic controllers that they were running out of fuel. The brash New Yorkers were assertive by nature, and the pilots simply hinted at their problems, as was their culture. These examples show that, depending on culture, people may accept the advice or instruction from someone with positional power, even when they know it is wrong and could mean that they would lose their lives.

We may think that in a democratic western society we are exempt from these cultural effects because we have the freedom to voice our opinions. However, every organization has its own culture, and often the leader with the positional power will decide whether the environment will encourage healthy debate or expect silent compliance. I experienced a good example of this back in the days when I was in army basics in 1988. It was conscription time and all males had to do two years of service. In basic training (bootcamp) we were "broken down so we could be built up" into the mold that the army required. Several weeks into training we went out for the so-called bush phase. This entailed a week or two out in the bush where the training was stepped up several levels, with night marches, grueling PT sessions, little sleep and bush-combat lessons. Many of the activities were accompanied by a loud barrage of insults and put-downs by the training corporals, whom we had come to obey without question. A common command that had been drilled into us went something like this:

Corporal: "Platoon, do you see that tree?"

Platoon: "Yes, Corporal!"

Corporal: "When I look again, you will be at that tree! Ready, GO!"

And off we went, running toward this revered tree, or leaf, or truck, or whatever. It was done without question. On one particular occasion in bush phase, we were marching through the veld when a big snake slithered through the grass ahead of us and straight into a large pile of broken branches. One of the corporals, presumably as a joke, grabbed one of the young troops and shouted: "Do you see that snake?"

"Yes, Corporal!"

"When I look again you will have fetched it for me! Ready, GO!"

Without question, the troop dropped his kit, ran up to the woodpile and was about to dive in and fetch the snake. Luckily, he was apprehended by a bunch of the training corporals who realized that this could spell trouble for them if he got hurt. They never thought the troop would actually do it! He was suitably reprimanded by the corporals for following orders. Yup, it didn't always make sense.

However, the point that this story makes, is that the influence that comes with a position is immense, especially in environments where openly questioning or disobeying superiors is condemned. Even in environments where questioning is allowed, the opinion of the person in the room who is highest on the company totem pole will often carry more weight than anyone else's. This is predominantly subconscious, but good leaders will be aware of this and actively remind their people to treat the leader's opinion with the same weight they would treat all other opinions. They would not only do this with words, but importantly also with actions.

In your leadership journey, especially when you are unfamiliar with being in charge, always remember your positional influence. Yesterday, when you were just part of the team, your opinion had a certain amount of sway. Today, as a respected leader, that same opinion may count for more in the minds of your team members. Remember Trump and his controversial suggestion about injecting disinfectant? When your crazy-scheme neighbor tells you this you'd laugh it off, but when the President of the USA says it, people begin to wonder... Always remember your words will cause people to act, so choose them wisely.

Culture: Why is this the way we do things?

Management consultant, Peter Drucker, famously said, *"Culture eats strategy for breakfast."* He did not mean that strategy is unimportant, but that culture was a more powerful force to implement lasting organizational success. It also means that if your culture does not support your strategy, the strategy is hampered at best and often simply doomed to fail.

What exactly is culture, though? Googling "What is company culture?" gave me 2.2 billion hits. That either means that everybody knows what it is, or nobody is exactly sure. For our purposes, let's simplistically define culture as "the way we do things". Sports teams, organizations, churches, nations, communities and even families have cultures. Some organizations are formal, others are on a first-name basis from day one. Some churches are bouncy and loud, while others are traditional. If you are living with your parents, and there is an 11pm curfew in place, you will know how strongly it is enforced. I have German heritage, and I'm always amazed at how efficiently the Germans can implement even large-scale changes. All of these are examples of culture.

Where does culture come from? In my opinion, culture will always come from the person or team that is in charge. This happens on small and large scale. A practical example is that of an honest versus dishonest person running a business. A person who prides himself on being honest at home in the small things and big things, will be very unlikely to be involved in large-scale fraud at work. Of course, I am assuming an average person, not a sociopath.

By the same token, a person who won't think twice about cheating his neighbor out of something, will most likely run his company the same manner—by cutting corners in various ways.

The honest versus dishonest example may or may not be the best one, since cultural differences are not good or bad in and of themselves. An example would be a culture of formality versus a culture of familiarity.

Here in South Africa we are emerging from a decade of so-called "state capture" under Jacob Zuma, where national funds were funneled into various international individuals' bank accounts via convoluted contracts and practices. This was a culture of corruption and self-interest, which could then easily be adopted by people who supported that. In organizations, the leader of the organization will determine what the culture of the organization will be. The reasons for this go back to earlier sections describing role models and positional power.

If the leader has a certain culture, it will not take long before the team around the leader will adopt a similar culture. This occurs by people adapting to the status quo and making shifts within themselves. However, if

> *"The most common form of discrimination is treating everyone the same."*

the culture violates an individual's own beliefs they might leave, either because they feel uncomfortable and frustrated or are being deliberately worked out. Obviously, the exfiltration of such people will aid in reducing the opposing view.

In an online discussion a few years ago, a concept was discussed that is related to this point. It said, *"The most common form of discrimination is treating everyone the same."* As it relates to organizational culture, there are people you naturally click with and understand. There are others with whom you have to be more deliberate in understanding their point of view, and still others who really challenge your views, requiring additional energy. It is important to accommodate all types to get a well-rounded view and a robust team. If, however, you treat everyone the same, you will treat them in the way that most suits *you*, and the people who thrive most in that environment are, by no surprise, the people who think most like you.

John Maxwell's book[9], *There's No Such Thing as "Business" Ethics*, explains the value of the international golden rule in business, namely, to do unto others as you would have done unto you. I believe it to be good advice. It cuts out double standards. Do we treat our suppliers as we would like to be treated by our customers? Do we treat our employees the way we would like to be treated by our superiors? Questions like these make for better decision-making. However, when we reconsider the title of Maxwell's book, we must realize there are no such thing as "business" ethics. Only ethics. In particular, the leader's ethics. By these the company will be known.

I was involved in a company where one of my tasks was to establish the values of the business in line with a positive mindset change. In the executive meeting we had a number of round-table discussions going from the usual initial list, to a more in-depth questioning of what each value really meant to each individual. We eventually reduced the list to four values, which then required another proper think-through.

However, before we could do this, I had a chance conversation with the owner about an issue of financial controls in which he informed me that he had decided to adopt a style of control where he believed that everyone would steal from the company if given the chance to do so undetected. I must stress here that the owner is not a hard, autocratic leader at all, and the controls were reasonable, but believing everyone would steal if given the chance went against one of the four values, namely *trust*. I'm not saying that when we trust people we don't have to put in controls. I am saying we cannot choose to trust and at the same time believe everyone will steal if given the chance. That effectively changed the nature of the values-definition project.

The take-away here is twofold. Firstly, we are formed by the culture in which we grow up, and the organizational cultures in which we work. Being aware of these cultures and questioning what they require us to believe is important to our leadership development. Secondly, as leaders in our teams, departments or companies, the internal culture which we bring to our people will impact them, and potentially their careers. Our culture is defined by our basic beliefs. Once again, I believe that being aware of this and making adjustments where necessary are the responsibility of every leader.

Your Turn

1. Which mantras have you grown up with that are significant for you?

_____

_____

_____

_____

_____

_____

2. What have you experienced with people in a position of power?

_____

_____

_____

_____

_____

_____

_____

3. Which organizational culture are you most comfortable with? How would you instill that culture?

_____

_____

_____

_____

ADDITIONAL THOUGHTS

We are not clean slates

By the time we are, say, twenty years old, we have thought many things, we have adopted various beliefs, consciously or subconsciously, and we have also experienced many situations. Throw all these together into the melting pot of our lives, and we will realize that we are not even close to being clean slates. Some people will have better tools in their leadership toolbox, others will have old, rusty ones that have to be thrown out. Some people may not even be interested in knowing they have a toolbox at all.

But if you are to be effective, in life and leadership, knowing what is in your toolbox and knowing whether your tools are helpful can make all the difference! Weldon Long[10], in his inspiring account, *The Power of Consistency*, calls this "inspecting the junk in your trunk". That's exactly what it is.

This is where our first real decision points emerge. When we are at the start of our career and we eagerly anticipate the future that lies ahead of us, we need to start deciding which roads to take, which concepts we buy into and, ideally, where we would like to end up. Some of us, like me, will only grasp the importance of those decisions many years later, but some of you may be far more intentional. But, with our imperfect slates and disparate toolboxes, off we go down the road, where various decision points await…

Your Turn

1. Which potentially false beliefs have you identified?

_____

_____

_____

_____

_____

_____

_____

PART B:
DECISION POINTS — THE INTERNAL CHOICES

"There comes a certain moment in everyone's life, a moment for which that person was born. That special opportunity, when he seizes it, will fulfil his mission—a mission for which he is uniquely qualified. In that moment, he finds greatness. It is his finest hour."

— Winston Churchill

I'm not certain that I entirely agree with Churchill that there is only a single moment. I believe that there are a multitude of key moments in our lives that will define who we are—as people and as leaders. The more we are aware of these moments as they happen, the more we can learn about ourselves. We open ourselves up to growth when we reflect back on these moments and how we responded to them. The good news is that no matter whether we have succeeded or failed in these moments, we will always learn.

These moments are our decision points.

All of us interact with people all the time. We have bosses, colleagues, team members, subordinates, friends, and family members. We deal with people every day. Some of my decision points have been the realization of my own emotions when someone had treated me or someone else in a particular way, and making a mental note of either including or excluding that treatment from my toolkit. This is an incredibly powerful way of learning *before* making the same mistakes.

As we build up our experience, we naturally begin to emerge as the leaders we aspire to be. We would then also seek opportunities to lead in organizations or situations that are best suited to our style and ability. If we do this long enough, I believe we will certainly be afforded those special opportunities that Sir Winston Churchill refers to. But we have to do the legwork in order to prepare. Key ingredients for accepting the learnings from these decision points are accepting and believing the fact that we have the power to *choose* a response, and that we are not purely wired for a certain reaction.

My decision points have come at random times. Sometimes they were out of the blue, other times out of long deliberation. Sometimes they were huge and dramatic, other times it only occurred to me after the fact that one had happened. Some were pleasant, while others were awkward and messy. Some I can look back on with satisfaction, others with regret. However, each of these points challenged me and forced me to ask myself what my priorities were, and what I would like to be known for. While your decision points might look different to mine, the fundamental questions are the same. I believe all leaders will have to face these questions multiple times in their journey.

In Part A, the frame of reference topics that had shaped my thinking were described. Now it's time to make some conscious decisions about what I will become. Decision points always involve an active choice, a choice that *we* make. Even if we "go with the flow" of whatever the prevailing thinking is, we are still *choosing* to do so. Author and motivational speaker, Bob Proctor, puts it like this:

> *"Life either happens by design or default, you choose."*

My decision points fell into three basic categories, namely foundational, character and behavioral decision points.

1. **Foundational** decision points. The decisions that are at my very core; convictions and beliefs that I have chosen and that I effectively bet my life on. This is *why* I exist.

2. **Character** decision points. The decisions that have shaped my values and ethics and are strongly informed by the foundational beliefs. This is *what* I stand for.

3. **Behavioral** decision points. These are the decisions that formed the basis of my leadership style and expression. They are in alignment with the foundational beliefs and character traits, but the decision outcome could be dependent on current circumstances. This is *how* I show up.

FOUNDATIONAL DECISION POINTS

T he foundational decision points are the decisions I make that are at my very core. They are the convictions and beliefs that I have chosen, and that I effectively bet my life on. This is *why* I exist.

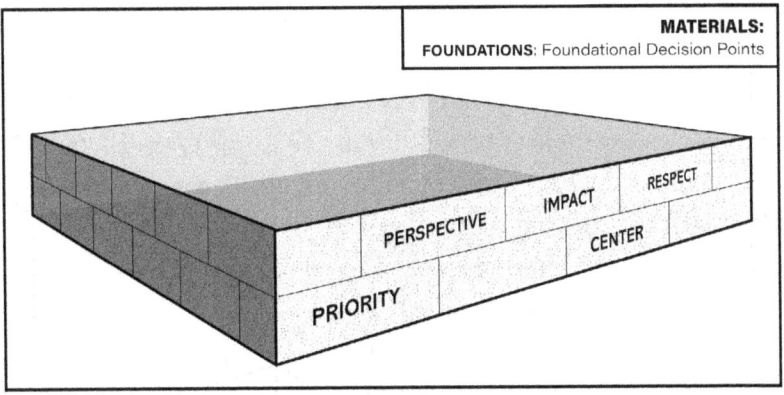

MATERIALS:
FOUNDATIONS: Foundational Decision Points

PERSPECTIVE

IMPACT

RESPECT

CENTER

PRIORITY

Impact: Play to Win or Play Not to Lose?

This may sound a bit like competing with others, but it isn't. It's about how we are going to run our own personal life race. Here we have to make the decision whether we are going to take risks to make some form of impact or play it safe and follow a seemingly predictable path to do "just okay" at the end. This decision does not only relate to financial aspects, but rather includes all those areas where we can either do what's enough or put ourselves out there—such as reputation, effort, service, commitment to causes that we feel strongly about, and many others.

I suppose this could be related to the so-called abundance versus scarcity mindset. I'll acknowledge it here, and then purposely move away from it because it means a variety of things to different people. Let me rather use an example of two different thinking styles. If you take a snapshot of where your life—in all its aspects—is right now, and then look at where you would see yourself in five years' time, there are two distinct ways of looking at it: playing not to lose, and playing to win.

Playing not to lose. In this way, you would look at the current circumstances in your life, and based on what you know, what you could reasonably accomplish, and what circumstances you anticipate, you could make an estimation of where you could *reasonably* expect to find yourself in five years' time. You would not take any massive risks because you have a plan and it is reasonable.

You could almost guarantee where you will end up, barring some major unforeseen life events.

Playing to win. In this way, you would forget where you are now. Imagine what you would like to achieve in all areas of your life, the things that energize and light you up, the impact you would like to make on the world around you. These are your dreams. Once you have these well-defined, then assess where you are now and work out the next couple of steps that need to be taken. You cannot plot the entire course, because by definition, you don't know what it is yet—you haven't done this before. It's riskier, will involve failure, and will require personal growth... and then some more personal growth.

Neither one of these approaches is wrong in itself. It is obvious that the playing-to-win approach is at the heart of what inspires us as humans, though. It's at the heart of all human progress and achievement. This isn't a new idea either. George Bernard Shaw said, *"The man who listens to reason is lost: Reason enslaves all whose minds are not strong enough to master her."*

Les Brown, motivational speaker, exhorts people with, *"You have greatness within you"* and *"Shoot for the moon, and even if you miss you will be among the stars."*

Now this doesn't mean you flaunt all thoughts of risk in every decision—even the playing-to-win philosophy will need robust plans to see it through. But it does change how you show up in the world every day.

My father had a very strong playing-not-to-lose philosophy, and on the face of it I can't say that I blame him. He was a German citizen who grew up in Holland,

and at the start of WWII his family was thrown out of the country with what they could carry, since Holland had decided to be neutral. They settled in southern Germany and during the war he turned 16, so he was drafted into the "Katastrofendienst" (Catastrophe Service) where he had to recover bodies from the rubble after each night's bombing raids by the Allied Forces. Tough job at 16! He was then reassigned to the Russian front, but fortunately the war had ended before he arrived. After spending the next six months as a prisoner of war under the British, he was released. His attempts at studying what he wanted to were blocked by the German government due to him having grown up in Holland and therefore being classed as a "foreign" German. So, he studied in the arts. In the 1950s he moved to South Africa, and after a long and successful career at the national broadcaster, retired comfortably. He didn't take risks. He simply made sure he kept his head down and diligently did what was required. It's understandable that, after experiencing so much loss, he would wish for a predictable outcome. But I didn't experience him as the happiest of people. It was interesting that my German mother, who also had her own horror stories from the war, had a playing-to-win outlook. She always involved herself in many new and interesting things, always wanting to contribute. Again, we do have a choice in how we respond.

My father's advice to me was to get a good education, a good job with a big organization that had good medical and retirement benefits, and stick it out. At the age of 23, I had an engineering degree, a job with a big military armaments company, with all the required perks, and could even buy my first home. Over the next year or two, one question began to plague me, although I couldn't really articulate it at the time—what do you do with the rest of your life if you have reached all your "significance" goals by 24? If this was all there is to life, then it really is quite dreary and tremendously uninspiring. I kept looking for new things to do, but always within the confines of the secure conditions required by my mindset. I did well, even finishing my M.Sc. in engineering and ending up on the board of a medium-sized manufacturing company, interestingly as the human resources director. At this point though, at 38 years of age, I got to the "significance" question again, and after many sleepless nights, prayers and mental pro's and con's charts, I decided that I needed to commit myself to finding the work that I was put on this earth to do. I was not content with merely playing not to lose in my life—I wanted to win, by finding and doing the best I could with what I had been given. To do this, I needed a clean break, and with a modest nest egg, lots of faith (see the "Perspective" decision point) and a mountainous helping of naiveté, I resigned without another job, and decided to see "what was out there". I intended to start something of my own, but had to first challenge the need for security that had been drummed into me. Just for context, I did have the usual bills— the mortgage for the house on the golf estate, the vehicle, the daughter in a private school—but I had my family's support, and off I went. This has led to a wild and fantastic adventure, lots of failures, lots of growth, and lots of impact with people in the area that has developed into being my niche—leadership development and coaching. Only in 2013, a full eight years after making this decision, did I discover that coaching was a formal career, even though it's what I had always been doing as my primary leadership style.

This adventure is far from over, and I suspect it won't be until the day I die. I am eternally grateful that I was prompted to make that decision, though, because it has led to the most fulfilling moments in my life, and often also the most financially insecure times as well.

There is a lot to learn from just that statement.

As an interesting point, it may simply be a case of birds of a feather, but in my coaching work with serious business owners, I have not come across a single one that has a play-not-to-lose approach. They all play to win. Being a business owner is not an easy task and requires constant growth.

Where do you stand on this foundational decision? How do you see the next five years of your life unfolding? Does it fill you with joy and energy, or more of a countdown-to-the-end feeling?

YOUR TURN

1. Will you play to win, or will you play not to lose?

_____

_____

_____

_____

2. What (and where) will you be in five years' time?

_____

_____

_____

_____

_____

_____

3. What are the next two steps you need to take to get there?

- Step 1

_____

_____

_____

- Step 2

_____

_____

_____

Importance Scoring (1-10) _____

Respect: All or Only Some?

Whether we like it or not, we are all prone to respecting some people more than others. Not because of what they have or have not done, but because of our own perceptions and, possibly, prejudices. When it comes to people we interact with regularly, some subtle shifts in respect reveal what is at the foundation of our behavior. Often, these shifts in showing respect are expected and, therefore, acceptable. VIP's usually expect better treatment and get it.

Respect all. Respecting everybody as a human being in their own right. When you have a respect-all mindset, then you acknowledge that you can learn something from everybody, irrespective of their position relative to yours. You acknowledge that you can contribute to those same people with your knowledge or experience. Respecting all for who they are also implies that you respect yourself for who you are.

Respect some. This mindset means we prioritize our respect for different people. For example, we could have more respect for the senior people in the organization and less respect for the junior people. If we are climbing the company ladder, we would perhaps look to impress the boss, and de-prioritize impressing the people who report to us. If people with a big title come and visit, we tend to roll out the full treatment, while others get a lesser response. The way we then view the people "right at the bottom" would be very different from how we view the company CEO. The degree to which we do this reveals how we expect other people to treat us as we climb the ladder. Often, it's

> *"While there's nothing wrong with having a nice parking spot, if it causes you sleepless nights and defines your worth, you have a problem!"*

institutionalized in the form of corner offices, secretaries, parking spots and the like. While there's nothing wrong with having a nice parking spot, if it causes you sleepless nights and defines your worth, you have a problem!

The respect-some mindset is very common, and I find it quite disturbing. While working with a particular executive, our team meeting went over time by nearly two hours. When I excused myself to go to the bathroom, I saw the exec's teenage son in the reception area. I asked if he was okay and whether he needed something. He simply replied that his dad had asked him to see him at the time the meeting was supposed to end. I apologized for the meeting having taken so long and he simply said, "It's okay, I'm used to it." Walking away from that interaction, I felt that, as a parent, I hope my daughter never has to feel that way about me. A similar incident occurred when I told one of the owners of a company that someone was waiting for him. When he asked who it was and I revealed it was one of the floor workers, his response was, "Oh, he can wait." No doubt, if it had been a shareholder, a customer, or any other VIP, the response would have been very different. Of course people have to wait sometimes, but the attitude that it's okay for me to waste your time, based on my assessment of your importance, is simply not warranted. Apologies ahead of time should count for all. As you might have guessed, I'm a bit of a stickler for meetings to start and end on time, and for people to be on time, purely because a lack of punctuality implies disrespect for other people.

On the other hand, if you respect all people, some wonderful things can happen. On a consulting project at a large electricity utility company, I met a cleaner, Elizabeth. She was an older lady and had a wonderful attitude. When she came in to clean the open plan offices, she used to encourage each of us, telling us what a great job we were doing. She wouldn't hear of us doing anything to help her, like getting up and out of her way, or moving papers so she could wipe the desks. One day I saw her in the corridor, and after introducing myself, I complimented her on this exceptional and different attitude and asked her where it originated from. She answered, "I'm not an educated or clever woman, but I know that electricity is important for the country. So, what you guys are doing must be important to make that happen. It's my job to make sure I clean up around you to the best of my ability and make it easier for you to do your job well. I can also encourage you. Then the company can do well, and I can earn money with which I am putting my children through university." I've been studying leadership for a long time, and Elizabeth the cleaner is still amongst my top examples of what a true leadership heart looks like. However, I would have completely missed that learning had I not respected her enough to first notice her attitude, and then taken the time to enquire about it.

There is also a third option: "Respect none." This is where someone has the seemingly intelligent premise that everyone around them has to earn their respect before they would give it. The problem is that it often goes together with the unspoken demand that others must respect *them* unconditionally. It's a double standard that will eventually become a respect-some decision.

It's clear that the decision of respecting all versus respecting some is foundational in how you function as a leader.

List all the people whom you interact with regularly, and then try and gauge your level of respect for each of them. Are they different? If so, why? What would you have to give up in order to highly respect *all* people?

YOUR TURN

1. Will you respect all people, or only those whom you perceive to be worthy?

_____

_____

2. How is your respect for others practically displayed?

_____

_____

_____

_____

_____

_____

_____

Importance Scoring (1-10) _____

Center: To Serve or to Be Served?

Copernicus was a European mathematician and astronomer who lived in the early 16th century. He calculated and proposed that the Earth revolved around the sun, rather than the Earth being the center of the then-known universe. While today it is a proven fact, it took several centuries for the church, which labelled the theory a heresy, to accept its science.

The "Center" decision point establishes who is at the center of your universe. Is it you, being served by others, or do you place others where you can serve them?

The term servant-leader has gained popularity, but not necessarily with all leaders. At the heart of this question is the motivation behind wanting to lead. It could even be asked whether leadership is seen as a career or a calling. This decision is closely linked with the "Respect" decision point, because to serve people willingly and well, you have to respect them. But respect can be done from a distance, almost passively, while serving is initiating and active. Serving means to roll up your sleeves and get into the thick of things.

To be served. Leading in this sense is about climbing a hierarchy in order to achieve more for oneself. When I am the boss, I get more respect, power, money, and so forth. I may well be an effective leader to a point, but when the personal rewards run out, or when a sacrifice needs to be made, I bail. Some might call this a wise career choice.

To serve. Leading in this sense is about having the best interests of the people you serve at heart. If they are individuals who report to you, you will do what you can to enable them to do their jobs better. You will develop and mentor them to be impactful, not only in their job functions, but as people. You will be inspired by their achievements more than your own. A wonderful example of this is Mother Teresa, who lived only to serve all people she interacted with, and serving often meant cleaning up in the kitchen after her nuns. In the 1990s she was arguably the most influential person on the planet as a result of her extreme servant heart.

There are many ways to serve, and most people will happily serve in some way and to some degree. But how far will you go to serve? I have had the privilege of working with various companies that have done wonderful things for their people and their families, or sponsored projects for communities, like schools or feeding schemes, and various other giving projects. These projects are normally funded from available profits and usually require employees to give some of their time.

Jacques du Preez of Intellinexus, a big-data IT consultancy, set up his company from the start as a company that serves. It is part of the company's DNA. The ownership of half the company went to a non-profit organization that did service projects, while the rest of the shares belonged to Du Preez and the later co-owners. The purpose of the IT consultancy is to provide excellence to its customers, just like any other

> *"The culture is to serve. It's what Intellinexus does, regardless of the circumstances."*

consultancy, but with the aim of generating profits that would be channeled into service projects that are completely divorced from IT. Intellinexus employees are also encouraged to give time to these projects. Practically, this structure may not necessarily generate more money or time than the previous examples, but the difference here is *intent*. It is part of the building blocks of the company, and not something that only happens if certain other conditions are met. You can imagine the culture that is being built within that company as a result.

Even during the COVID-19 crisis in 2020, which also affected Intellinexus negatively, the company started a fund that would match the monetary donations made by its employees to a designated feeding charity. In addition, qualifying Intellinexus customers who were negatively affected by the pandemic were offered a limited amount of no-cost consulting time to keep things on track, and employees contributed to this in the form of time worked. The culture is to serve. It's what Intellinexus does, regardless of the circumstances. Keep in mind that this was against the backdrop of the company having to reduce all its costs and overheads to survive the pandemic's economic effects.

It is a rare privilege to work with a leader, and company, of this caliber.

What does being a servant-leader mean to you? Is it an idea that excites you, or does it put you off? How do you respond internally when your people achieve great results that don't credit you?

YOUR TURN

1. Who will be at the center of your universe, in other words, who will you serve?

_____

_____

_____

2. What attitudes will you need to change to serve?

_____

_____

_____

Importance Scoring (1-10) _____

Priority: People First or Finance First?

Regardless of the industry, the size of the company, or the state of the bank balance, this is a foundational decision that every organizational leader will face at some point. It is also a decision that everybody with a job will be affected by at some point in their careers. It is a complicated decision because both people and finances are important, and they are also interlinked—you can't really have one without the other. The topic here is not so much about what to do, but more about our base motivation when making this decision. That base motivation will determine, amongst others:

- Staff incentives and their conditions
- Staff increases
- Staff lay-offs or retrenchments
- Profit-share percentages

It's no question that company health and profitability are important, and the survival of a company is crucial to the well-being of its employees. On the extremes of this decision are two dangerous situations, and I will use lay-offs, or retrenchments, as the example.

The finance-first extreme. In his book, *I have the watch*, Jon S Rennie[11] makes an interesting statement. He suggests that the standards of accounting themselves have led to an unfortunate imbalance between finance and people. Loosely put, in financial statements, equipment and buildings are seen as assets—in other words, things that have value and can be put to work to earn money. On the other hand, people and all their associated costs are seen as liabilities—things that cost money and should be reduced. While this may be an over- simplification of the many complexities of this situation, my experience in some exco's is that cost reductions start by focusing on the biggest liability, which is invariably staff costs and overheads. It starts becoming this big number that must be reduced at all costs, irrespective of the damage it causes people. This is the extreme—when we lose sight of the people behind the numbers and can only see resources and financial results. In some countries it is legal to lay people off in order to achieve the profitability targets that have been promised to shareholders, often accompanied by bonuses for the executives who achieved those targets.

One does not have to look very hard to find that this is an extreme finance-first motivated decision.

The people-first extreme. In this extreme, organizations fail to use lay-offs and retrenchments, even past the point of it being a last resort, leading to the business being severely damaged or even destroyed. No matter how people-focused one is, allowing the company—on which many people depend—to go under by failing to implement necessary measures, is negligent at best. A good example of this is underperforming government departments that are overstaffed, but no action is taken to reduce staff. While the motivation for this may be more political, the outcome is the same. If it were a private company, it would collapse. If this does happen in a private company, in my opinion, it is due to an owner or leader that is not prepared to make good decisions, probably for personal or emotional reasons, such as avoiding discomfort and blame.

However, between the extremes is a vast grey area that potentially masks our priorities, and is open to manipulation. Here we have leaders who have a leaning towards one side or the other, who must balance keeping the company viable with losing people who are potentially friends or even family. It's within this area that the people-first versus finance-first decision comes to the fore.

As individuals, we are brought up with certain beliefs about money. A common false belief connects having lots of money with some form of dishonesty, while being poor and hard-working is somehow more noble. This belief can potentially undermine a sound business decision because "finance first" is seen as being greedy and "wrong".

I have personally been through several downsizing, right-sizing, or cost-cutting retrenchment processes. In some cases, I have been retrenched. In other cases, I have been retained. Sometimes these processes have been quick and painless, and others have lasted for 18 months. At times, I have been responsible for putting together name lists of my colleagues for possible retrenchments, and on two occasions I led large-scale retrenchment programs and was the chief negotiator with several militant unions. I have sat and cried with friends that I have had to let go, and I have had to rebuild the trust of others who have stayed. I have received commendations of leading retrenchment processes well. I have also received berating phone calls from people whom my decisions have affected, or their families. No matter how you look at these processes, they are upsetting.

Retrenchments can result in cleaning house, cutting out deadwood, or correcting things that have evolved due to standards and discipline not having been enforced. However, the finance-first view is to welcome retrenchments as an excuse to achieve that. The people-first view is to use retrenchments as a very last resort to save a business. I have worked with owners who have had the correct rationale for implementing retrenchments but have actively looked for ways to avoid them. In some cases, they have been successful and saved several people from unnecessary hardship.

When it comes to salary and contract negotiations, I have encountered interesting responses, again based on the finance-first versus people-first mindsets. I have been involved in companies where employees had to fight tooth and nail for every bit of salary concession they got. The owners were working on the basis of getting as much as they can for as little as possible money. I have also worked with the opposite, where companies insisted on paying people according to their value, irrespective of what they had asked for. I've been in exco's where people had to negotiate for salary decreases because the owners valued them highly. In one memorable example, I was paid three times what I had asked, because the client refused to pay me too little.

I have to say here that the success of the companies, whether people-first or finance-first, was not hugely different. The only difference was the priority they put on people. In *Leadership and Self-deception,* a business novel written by researchers at the Arbinger Institute[12], the case is made that we can see people either as people, or as resources. If we see them as people, we will see them with their families, dreams, hurts and frustrations, and we will consider how we can help them. If we see them as resources, we only see how they can help us and what they can do for us. They further illustrate that all of us do both at varying times. Just think of that slow driver in front of you when you are in a hurry to get to an appointment. Our reaction, or action, will stem from how we see that driver—as a person with all the usual imperfections, or as a blockage to what we want to achieve. I've done both. Often, on the same day!

In the same vein, Bob Burg[13] and John David Mann talk about the finance-first versus people-first decision in their business novel, *The Go-Giver*. In the story, a salesperson asks whether a particular product makes money. The mentor answers, *"That is a bad first question.*

> *"If a business is not about the people it serves, including the people it employs, it is missing something."*

The first question is whether it serves the needs of the customer." Only once that has been firmly established, should the question be asked whether it makes money.

As far as my intentional, foundational belief goes, my personal decision within this area is firmly: people first. As far as I'm concerned, if a business is not about the people it serves, including the people it employs, it is missing something. I question why it even exists. Extreme? Possibly. But it's how I think.

How will your belief shape the company you may build or run in the future?

YOUR TURN

1. Will you put people first or finance first?

_____

_____

_____

_____

2. How will your decision shape the company you may build or run in the future?

_____

_____

_____

_____

_____

_____

_____

Importance Scoring (1-10) _____

Perspective: Eternal or Earthly?

This particular decision point remains my most important one, the one from which all my other decisions flow. For me, having an eternal versus earthly perspective is solidly a faith-based decision. For you, it may not be. Then I would encourage you to see this foundational decision point in the context of making decisions for a cause greater than yourself, a legacy, or a higher goal, even if you don't believe in the existence of God.

I have an eternal perspective, which results in a mostly positive outlook on life. This is not a blind optimism, but an optimistic view that chooses to believe in a positive outcome. It is best described by the Stockdale paradox. Admiral James Stockdale was a US Navy pilot and Vietnam prisoner of war for over seven years, and attributed his survival to a mixture of faith and pragmatism. In the book, *Good to Great*, written by Jim Collins, this became known as the Stockdale paradox:

> *"Retain the faith that you will prevail in the end, regardless of the difficulties, and at the same time confront the most brutal facts of your current reality, whatever they might be."*

My calm positivity in certain situations can freak some people out. Some will say, "We have to be realistic here." Have you noticed how, when people say that, that they always go to the negative? It's always in response to someone who chooses to be positive. While I may need a dose of realism now and then, a positive outlook, without ignoring the current brutal facts, is a much more creative state from which to work.

However, let me be specific about what this decision means to me. How I view my life in terms of God, the universe, the past, the present and the future—and how strongly I hold that viewpoint—has a massive impact on all other decisions.

Eternal perspective. With an eternal perspective, you believe that the time you have on this earth is very short, and simply serves as a step to an eternal life with God. Your experience of the eternal life is dependent on the way you live, what you believe, and how you conduct yourself in this life. The decisions and examples you set in this life have massive implications for you and others in the eternal life. As a result, you are able to face hardships and self-sacrifice in this life, because you are working for a higher goal. Having an eternal perspective does not make you a good person, it simply acknowledges a Higher Power.

Earthly perspective. With an earthly perspective, this life is all there is. What you achieve or fail to achieve in this life has no lasting effect, and therefore you may work hard to win in this life. The need for wealth, health, power and pleasure is all for an earthly experience, and once you reach the end of the road, that's it. Morals and ethics similarly are simply bound by the consequences that can occur on this earth, with no lasting effect. Whether you are a nice guy—or a tyrant—is a decision based on what you want out of this life, balanced with how much empathy you have for fellow human beings. Having an earthly perspective does not make you a bad person, it simply means that you believe there is no eternal consequence.

Under the "Impact" decision point, I described how, after repeatedly getting to the question of significance in various positions I had held, I decided to "play to win" and do the work I was put on this earth to do. That statement is already a clue to an eternal perspective, but the background story of how I arrived at making the decision to play to win lies in first having made this "Perspective" decision.

Beryl Donkin was a biochemist and teacher, and in her early fifties became a Methodist minister in the church that I attended in Pretoria. This was around 2005—15 years before writing this book. Beryl's sermons resonated with me more and more, and there was one in particular that started a thinking process in me that would change my life. I was a Christian. I believed that Jesus Christ is the Son of

God and that He had given up His life for mine on the cross. I knew about the eternal life, but I'm not sure I quite grasped the connection between how we live this life and the eternal life. The sermon, as I remember it, went something like this:

Beryl described life as studying for a Biology exam. You go through the notes, you learn the concepts. Then you work hard at all the diagrams, drawing them out over and over until you know them well. After hours and hours of painstaking study, you finally walk into the classroom to face the panel of lecturers who will test you. They ask whether you studied, and you tell them about all the studying you've done, how you went through the Biology textbooks, learnt the diagrams, practiced them over and over until you were completely ready.

> *"We are not on this earth by accident, we have a specific role to play."*

"That's very commendable," they say, "but why did you do that?"

"In order to get the best possible Biology test score I could," you answer.

Then they reply, "But this is a Mathematics exam."

Beryl went on to explain that God has a plan and purpose for our lives. It doesn't matter how hard you work, if you're not listening to God's leading, you may be following the wrong plan. By not following the plan He has for your life, you will miss out on the many rewards and blessings God has for you, and others, both on earth and in heaven. We are not on this earth by accident, we have a specific role to play.

This sermon really spoke to me, and I could relate so well to having had success several times in my career, and at precisely those same times I would feel unfulfilled, and I would think that there has to be more. Over the next few months, I visited Beryl on numerous occasions, and she became a spiritual mentor to me. I struggled with the idea of hearing God's voice, and how to be led. After all, I was saved, and I did pray about stuff. What more was there? She introduced me to the "Lectio Divina", or "Divine Reading", a method of reading the Bible that was first practiced by the early Christians. She encouraged me to pray, read a portion of scripture, ponder and meditate on it, journal about it, pray some more. She explained that our subconscious mind and our imagination are also gifts from God, and He speaks to us through these. I was an engineer and I valued hard facts greatly, so I remember telling Beryl that I didn't buy any of this "new" method, but because I was desperate to hear from God, I would commit to doing it weekday mornings for the next six months. I further challenged God (respectfully) to speak to me in these six months so that I would know which direction to move in.

But it only took a month and I was sold. I was given such clear answers to some of my questions that it went beyond coincidence. I say "some" because I have a few questions that God is adamantly not answering yet, much to my frustration. Questions like, "Please, show me the master plan?" God still requires some faith from me, I guess. It was during this time that a single word from Beryl changed my outlook completely. One word. I had come to the conclusion that God was leading me to take a step in faith, to leave a permanent job and clear my slate, for Him to fill in the details of the life I was to lead for Him. But as I've mentioned before, my dad's example was one of hanging on to security, being safe, and not rocking the boat. God was asking me to drop all that and put all my eggs into His basket, so to speak. I grappled with the decision for a few weeks, and I told Beryl how I was agonizing and how scared I was of making the wrong decision.

"Why?" Beryl asked.

This stopped me in my tracks. *Why?* I was making this massive decision to walk away from security into the unknown, where failure meant a destitute family with nowhere to go, and Beryl asked why I'm scared! I thought she had lost it.

Then she said, "Don't you think God can work with a wrong decision?" I immediately had one of those "Duh!" moments and thought, Why didn't I think of that?

It was so obvious. The God who created and rules this universe can step into any situation, and if I was going to follow His plan for my life, I would need to have faith in that. I did take that step in faith and have built up my eternal perspective of life ever since. I still journal most weekday mornings, and this gives me clear and good direction in my life. It's not always easy, because many times I'm told to wait, and the situations are frustrating. Mistakes do get made, but God is always there to walk the road with me. After 15 years—and 24 journals, and counting—I still find this to be the most dependable decision-making process I know.

This was my journey. I'm not advocating that everyone now jump ship and follow my path step by step. God needed to free me from an over-dependence on earthly security, and that may not be your vice at this stage. I am advocating that, should you decide to have an eternal perspective, to seek God's path for your life and follow that.

I have been guided by the following two passages of Scripture in this regard, may they bring some guidance to you, too.

JOHN 15:5 (NKJV)

"I am the vine, you are the branches. He who abides in Me, and I in him, bears much fruit; for without Me you can do nothing."

Stay close to Him, first. The rest will follow.

EPHESIANS 2:10 (NIV)

For we are God's handiwork, created in Christ Jesus to do good works, which God prepared in advance for us to do.

There is a plan for my life, and He has prepared it that way.

By following this eternal-perspective guidance, I can accept situations as being a necessary part of a journey, rather than a failure that needs to be eradicated because I have lost ground on my earthly accumulation of whatever my interest is. I have encountered a myriad of situations, good and bad, that have all contributed to my learning. In addition, I have experienced a level of fulfilment that I had never encountered before.

Take a moment to ponder upon your life circumstances right now. How would having an eternal perspective change the decisions you need to make today?

YOUR TURN

1. Do you have an earthly or eternal perspective?

_____

_____

2. What would having an eternal perspective or higher goal mean to you?

_____

_____

_____

_____

_____

_____

Importance Scoring (1-10) _____

ADDITIONAL THOUGHTS

_____

_____

CHARACTER DECISION POINTS

Character decision points are what shape our values and ethics and are strongly informed by our foundational beliefs. This is *what* we stand for.

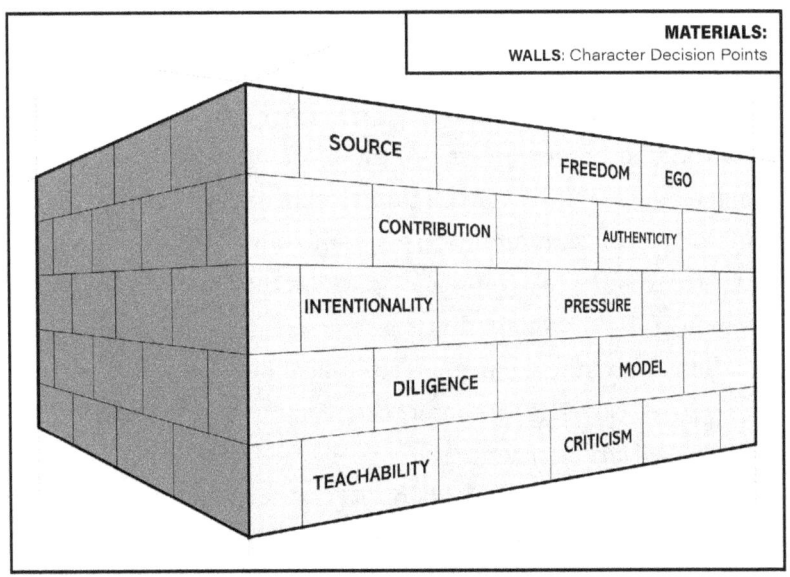

MATERIALS:
WALLS: Character Decision Points

SOURCE
FREEDOM   EGO
CONTRIBUTION   AUTHENTICITY
INTENTIONALITY   PRESSURE
DILIGENCE   MODEL
CRITICISM
TEACHABILITY

Contribution: Serving Down or Serving Up?

If it were up to me, I would turn all organograms upside-down. Of course, then I would have to redefine the name of this section, so for now, let's keep the organogram as is.

Who do you serve, and why? This is the core question of the "Contribution" decision. In traditional hierarchies, the supervisor reports to the manager, who reports to the senior manager, who reports to the executive—or some variation of this theme. Production or company results are measured, and rewards are awarded from the top down. The higher up we go, the more money we stand to make, and our lifestyle changes accordingly. In the vast majority of conversations about our work, we will typically refer to companies or bosses that *we work for*, and teams and individuals that *work for us*.

> *"As leaders we are not in charge of people, we have people in our charge."*

This may not seem to be a big deal, but I think it is. In the 2016 Live2Lead conference, Simon Sinek[16] said, *"As leaders we are not in charge of people, we have people in our charge."* This is the "Contribution" decision, and it has a massive impact on our focus in leadership.

Serving up. If I am a line manager, I will, by default, look to my boss as the person I work for, and will accordingly gauge whether I'm doing a good job by the feedback I get from my boss. Sometimes I will be evaluated based on what my team has managed to achieve. However, the primary and most important relationship in the pyramid is the me–my-boss relationship. If I have to do a task, my first thought might be, What does my boss want? I would want to do that to the best of my ability, because that's how I get the biggest reward.

Serving down. If I am a leader in that same situation, my primary function is to lead my team, in other words, the people who report to me. I always first ask how any course of action will affect the team, and then I ask what I need to do to serve them best. The task still needs to be done, but the development and success of my team are what matter. The reward is not what the boss gives me, it's what the team becomes and achieves. My evaluation is not what the boss thinks of my results, but what the team achieves and thinks of my leadership. The most important relationship in the pyramid is the my-team–me relationship. How did I help them improve? Where did I slow them down? These are the types of questions that should be foremost in my mind.

If you are uncomfortable with the idea of "serving" as a leadership principle, keep in mind that, as the leader, part of your service to the team would be to give guidance, discipline and reprimand where necessary, and to make the tough and unpopular decisions that are required for the team to operate at its best.

Do we serve a boss for personal reward, or do we serve a team for *its* development and the development of its members? If we serve the boss for personal reward, we tell the team to get the job done because the boss wants it so. If we serve the team, we ask the team what they need from us for them to accomplish the task. If we serve the boss, and a team member doesn't perform, we might want to replace them with a newer and more efficient "model". Whereas, if we serve the team, we ask the underperforming member whether they're okay, whether they are struggling with something, and whether we can help. If we are lucky, we work in a company where the two are synonymous. More commonly, though, they are at odds with each other and we will have to make a decision on who we serve.

At ABC Manufacturing* we had biannual performance appraisals. These were conversations with the boss where we went through our results and committed to what we would accomplish in the following six months. We would get scores based on our discussions, and bonuses were vaguely tied to that score. In preparation for these discussions, we had to fill in a one-pager to rate ourselves on our performance, list the challenges we had, and draw up goals for the following six-month period.

We had a team from a well-known consulting company working with us during one of these cycles. They were there to aid with a culture change from an autocratic leadership style to a participative leadership style. As part of their project, the consultants would sit in on our various production meetings and then give us pointers to improve. One morning, while we were having our foundry morning meeting, with consultant in place, I realized that my performance evaluation was straight after the meeting. I hadn't done the preparation for the meeting yet, although our goals were all fairly clear. The "Contribution" question was in my head, however, so I asked my team to fill out my one-pager for me, and I would take it to my boss for my evaluation, without any amendments. I wanted to know only one thing from them: How successfully had I led them in the last six months? I left the room and gave them 10 minutes to complete the form. When I returned, they gave me the form and I walked straight to my boss's office, without having read the input. The consultant stopped me.

"Are you going in there without reading the form?" he asked, quite incredulously.

"Yup," I said.

"What if they said things about you that will make you look bad?" he asked.

"If what they have said is true, then it's an area that I need to work on," I answered. "I'm here to lead this team, and they are in the best position to tell me whether I am doing a good job."

"That's a very brave move, but it could be stupid," he said.

I shrugged my shoulders and went in for my performance review. I don't think it went badly, because I don't really remember it. What I do remember, though, was how the relationship between my team and me shifted. I had trusted them with my review, potentially my bonus also, and I had specifically asked them to be truthful in their rating. I neither defended nor justified—I simply accepted their verdict. As a result, they knew that I took them and my role seriously, and that I was primarily there to serve them.

This was one of those decisions that I didn't plan. It took me by surprise because I had forgotten to prepare, but it led to a change of habit that has since been extremely valuable. I serve down first, and then up. In all of my positions after that, I have identified whom I should serve most, and have asked them for feedback. As a result, I have learnt quite a bit about myself, and managed to do my job more effectively.

In leadership lectures, I use the following comparison to show whom leaders should serve. Consider a pop diva doing a live show with an entourage of dancers and musicians. The show is centered around her, and the dancers are there purely to support and enhance that picture. This might be appropriate for a solo artist but it's not the picture of a serving-down leader. The picture of a serving-down leader is more like an orchestra. The orchestra is the team, the conductor is the leader, and the audience is the boss (or the customer). Note that the leader has his back to the boss. The leader is only interested in what the team is doing, ensuring that he gives them the best possible information to do a good, tight and coherent job. The team is focused on their individual jobs and can see the impact on the boss (or the customer). When the performance ends, the entire team receives the reward of applause from the audience.

If the conductor were overly concerned with the audience, he would keep looking to the audience to see whether they were enjoying the show. He would not serve the orchestra, mistakes would be made, and the performance would suffer. Likewise, a leader who is obsessed with pleasing his boss, and neglects to give his team proper direction, causes the entire team's performance to suffer. Sometimes even the individual team members are casualties.

What does your company hierarchy look like? Is there a clear distinction between serving up versus serving down? If so, what have you been doing up until now, and what will you do from now on?

YOUR TURN

1. Will you be serving up or serving down?

_____

_____

2. How will you implement your decision? Does the organization that you work for support this view?

_____

_____

_____

_____

_____

Importance Scoring (1-10) _____

Model: Example or Excuse?

What message do you send to those around you? Being a consistent example is crucial in building trust. This includes the way you deal with others in what you say and do, and how you balance needs and expectations in decision-making. Consistency makes the difference between being seen as a leader who makes up the rules as they go along, versus a leader who can be counted on to be as fair as possible in their treatment of others and situations.

Excuse. It is always easy to justify actions. Making sound decisions requires sound leadership, not because they are easy and obvious, but because there are multiple right answers. If you have been leading for a while, you will know that situations always give you the opportunity to justify your actions in a way that sounds reasonable to you. Self-justification is how people manage to get away with "odd" behaviors. The ultimate cop-out is the "that's just the way I am" excuse, where followers simply have to accept a decision or a behavior because the boss has a certain temperament. But as a follower, you have that nagging feeling that makes you wonder whether this leader can be trusted.

> *"Making sound decisions requires sound leadership, not because they are easy and obvious, but because there are multiple right answers."*

In the book, *Leadership Gold*, John Maxwell[17] declares that you will treat others based on their *results*, while you will treat yourself based on your *intentions*. We let ourselves off the hook easier than we let others off the hook. It's completely obvious here that if you are to be as effective a leader as possible, you can't have people wondering about how you would react in certain situations. Your people must know that you will always be consistent in how you treat others and yourself, and this builds trust.

If people trust you, they will follow you.

Example. In being consistent, there is also the great opportunity of modelling desired behavior. If you are visibly behaving in a particular way, then you can confidently require your people to do the same. People are always watching you and, as their leader, they will remember where your words and actions don't match up.

When I was the foundry manager at ABC Manufacturing*, I was challenged with the "Model" decision point. I rarely lose my temper, but one morning I was in the paint plant where one of the shift managers was showing me how the foundry's "poor workmanship" was causing them not to make their targets. We always tried to be reasonable in accepting this kind of criticism, but in this particular case I strongly felt that they were being completely unreasonable. So, next to the offending stack of products, a heated argument erupted, as it can only happen in a production plant. At one point, I took one of the products and threw it on the ground and stormed off, furious. By the time I got back to the foundry, the bush telegraph had already spread

> "Your people must know that you will always be consistent in how you treat others and yourself, and this builds trust."

the news of what had happened in the paint plant.

Several weeks later, one of my supervisors, Paul*, was charged with throwing a casting at one of the machine operators and injuring him. Paul was very competent and strict, and the union was keen to use this as a way to get rid of him. In the disciplinary enquiry it was clear that Paul hadn't thrown the casting at the operator at all. He had negligently dropped the casting, which had rolled down a couple of steps into the operator as he was walking past the staircase. The operator even acknowledged that was what had happened, and that he hadn't really been injured. However, Paul had been negligent, and according to the disciplinary code should get a warning. This was acceptable to him, and a formal warning would also stop the process in its tracks with a fair outcome that the union could not fight.

This was all good and well, except that what Paul had done was not any worse than what I had done in the paint plant a few weeks earlier. That incident was still fresh, and the foundry personnel don't forget this kind of incident, especially if you are standing up for them. It becomes one of those stories that start with "Remember the time when..." and then they would all nod enthusiastically. The problem was that I was uncomfortable with giving Paul a warning for something that I had also been guilty of but hadn't been reprimanded for. Even though I could justify it—I had been provoked, the paint plant supervisor was being unreasonable, I was defending my team, etc.—it still made me uneasy. All the various options milled through my mind while I was deciding what to do.

I gave my judgement to the participants in the hearing. Paul would be given the warning as we had agreed. He had been negligent, and that behavior needed correction. Then I asked them if they remembered the incident in the paint plant. They all smiled and said that they did. I asked whether it would be fair if Paul got a warning, but I didn't. Now they were almost laughing and said it probably wouldn't. So, we agreed that I would also be given a warning, which would go into my HR file, and then the matter would be settled. At this point, they were beside themselves—they got to give the boss a real warning! I printed out the paperwork for the two warnings, we signed them, and I got ready to take the papers to the HR department.

Here is the important point. As they filed out of my office, a junior manager came to me and quite thoughtfully remarked, "I really liked that." To me it was just a warning, but to that guy it was a defining moment, an example of what it means to lead with consistency. This story also did the rounds in the foundry, and I'd like to think that my people felt that they had a leader who would treat them the same way as he would treat himself—that they had a leader they could trust.

Maybe I am a slow learner, because that wasn't the last time that I gave myself a warning. From time to time I still transgressed, mostly inadvertently. When faced with the facts, I would give myself a warning and I would let my team know, so that they knew there were no double standards. It was an opportunity to model the correct behavior.

What behavior do you model? Do you apply standards to yourself that are different from the standards applied to others? What do you need to do?

YOUR TURN

1. Are you an example to your people, or will you make excuses?

_____

_____

2. What do you do to consistently model correct behavior?

_____

_____

_____

_____

Importance Scoring (1-10) _____

Teachability: Tell You or Teach Me?

One of the most debilitating things that a leader can do, is to stop being teachable. It annoys the team, it puts a lid on the capacity of the organization, and as far as being influential goes, it stops the leader dead in their tracks. If people are not heard, they close up and will not receive

> *"A leader who is not teachable is facing a character dilemma."*

a message as readily as they would, had they been included in the discussion.

Tell you. Aside from the influential effects, a leader who is not teachable is facing a character dilemma. If he is not teachable, it means that he feels he has all the answers, and nobody can teach him anything new. This is an attitude towards some, or all, other people that is blatantly disrespectful. Imagine if you had all the answers—you would need a *lot* of answers to say that nobody can teach you anything. All evidence points to the fact that one person cannot possibly know it all. It's an impossible, ludicrous belief, and still some leaders act in this way. It may be situational, where the leader feels their team can't teach them anything new, or someone with "lesser" credentials can't possibly contribute. Taken to extremes, every discussion becomes a debate where the leader just has to be right in order to validate their beliefs (and perhaps their status). The day the leader becomes unteachable, is the day they stop being an effective leader. I believe an extremely powerful antidote to this is having kids. When your six-year old teaches you something about flowers, love, patience or imagination—and you humbly realize what has just happened—you'll be back on the road to effectiveness.

Teach me. When you are put in charge of a new team, you will be faced with the teachability decision. It happens in a very subtle way that is easy to miss. Don't miss it, because it is an ideal opportunity to set the tone for your leadership. Picture the first meeting where some questions are posed on a problem in the plant, a crisis in sales—or whatever relevant context applies—and all heads turn to… you. Before you were the leader, this didn't happen. Now it does. You are expected to have the answers, so ingrained is our picture of an omniscient leader. What will you do? If you are inexperienced, you may feel the need to come up with some ideas and take the lead. You may even have some good ideas, but the problem is that your positional influence gets in the way, and your ideas automatically receive a higher weighting in the minds of your followers. Unless you have people in the team that will boldly question the ideas of authority figures, your idea will stick, irrespective of its true worth.

If, however, you want to build a team that is strong on providing robust solutions to problems, this is a golden opportunity. I've learned to say, "Stop looking at me like I have all the answers. If I did, we wouldn't need to meet." The playing field has now been levelled, and we can start debating. It is then crucial to allow every idea to be raised, because even zany ideas often spark effective solutions.

> *"Stop looking at me like I have all the answers. If I did, we wouldn't need to meet."*

When I started in the position of foundry manager, I learnt this in a practical way. My style was to think through the problem, mull over the possible solutions, often for days, and when I was sure that I had the answer, I would call the 12-person senior team together and proudly announce what I thought we should do and, by the way, I would welcome their input. As expected, my idea would be accepted, and we'd start planning. Fortunately, I had two managers who could be quite belligerent, and they would start questioning every aspect of my idea. It would take ages to debate everything with them, and the whole team, including me, would get quite frustrated with them. But in the end, their questions revealed flaws in the plan and the debating process would eventually result in a far more robust solution to the problem. Over time, I realized the value of these "difficult" people, and often discussed my ideas with them *before* opening up the debate to the bigger audience. It was just much more effective that way. I went from *telling* my team what to think, to *asking* them what they thought.

Teachability is a vital tool for any leader, sales professional, negotiator, or anyone else who regularly interacts with people. In his 1978 classic, *SPIN Selling*, Neil Rackham[18] explains the results of research involving 49 expert negotiators, where they compared their behaviors during negotiations. They highlight the value of listening and amending proposals and viewpoints in order to reach a successful conclusion.

From the research, it can be seen that expert negotiators spend 84.4% of their time asking questions. They do this by searching for relevant information, testing for understanding to ensure that they have understood people correctly and finding out about their negotiation partners' emotions and feelings. In contrast, they spend only 5.8% on making proposals and justifying them.

No	Behavior	Time
1	Search for information	35.5%
2	Testing for understanding	28.7%
3	Information on Emotions	20.2%
4	Predictions of behavior	10.7%
5	Irritating remarks	3.8%
6	Aggressive	3.2%
7	Reasons to substantiate statements	3.0%
8	Counter proposals	2.8%

To put it plainly, they spent 84% asking questions and listening, and only around 6% giving answers. An effective negotiator must be teachable in order to be good at his job. And leaders have to be good negotiators.

The "Teachability" decision point will surface multiple times. In any situation when you are asked for answers, and you don't readily have them, you have the option to either give a hasty opinion or say that you will get back to the enquirer. This may seem easy, but the context can be overwhelming. You may be asked a question as a consultant to a high-powered client. You may be asked to recommend a course of action by an impatient entrepreneur. Your team might need reassurance during tough times, or you may be asked a question by some people you desperately need to impress, either socially or professionally. As I've gained more experience, I've become more comfortable with admitting that I don't know, but I always come back with an answer after having been able to think it through. Where possible, I'd use the opportunity to probe the person asking the question, and as a team we would come up with a best course of action.

One of my consulting clients has even commented on the fact that I have the guts to say, "I don't know", and that they appreciated that about me.

How teachable are you? When you are asked for answers that you don't have, do you give your best guess, or do you include others to find out? If you would like to improve your teachability, how will you do that?

YOUR TURN

1. Do you have all the answers for the team, or do you ask the questions?

_____

_____

_____

_____

2. How teachable are you? When asking questions, how likely are you to really listen to the answers?

_____

_____

_____

_____

_____

3. How can you become more teachable?

_____

_____

Importance Scoring (1-10) _____

Authenticity: Open Book or Guarded Vault?

The subject of authenticity, specifically in leadership, has become very popular. It's clear that to inspire people to be at their best, we have to form authentic connections with them, which is difficult if we are playing some kind of "role". Unless we are dealing with a skilled manipulator, sociopath or conman, we usually have a sense of whether somebody is genuine or not. It may be obvious to state this, but true authenticity can only come from being authentic. Authenticity is not a tactic, and "fake it 'til you make it" is a doomed strategy. Authenticity is a character trait that is decided upon and practiced. In *The Go-Giver*, Bob Burg and John David Mann[13] establish five laws of success. One of them is the law of authenticity that states, *"The most valuable gift you have to offer is yourself."*

To be fully authentic takes vulnerability, courage and commitment. We have to open up completely but appropriately to people, allowing them to see our faults. This is both scary and liberating at the same time. Scary, because obviously we are opening ourselves up to rejection and ridicule, where we do not have an ounce of control over how people will react. Liberating, because once we are fully vulnerable, we have the strength to take on challenges, knowing that we

> *"It may be obvious to state this, but true authenticity can only come from being authentic."*

are operating from a solid foundation. There is no point in becoming vulnerable unless we plan on making changes in areas that we are dissatisfied with, and therefore we need the commitment to grow and improve.

In leadership, vulnerability and approachability are a powerful combination. I'm not even sure that they are that distinct from each other, since both have to do with connecting with other people. Vulnerability gives the example, approachability allows the connection, and then the influence is there. No amount of vulnerability will help if people are walking on eggshells around you.

Many people and leaders would shy away from raw authenticity for various reasons. Possibly it's too scary to go into some of the dark recesses and open them up to people. Perhaps those dark recesses have been repressed for too long and people are unable to be truly authentic with themselves. Or maybe people know that their motives are not as pure as they ought to be, but they don't feel the need to change.

At some point in your leadership journey you will have to make the character decision around authenticity. Will you be an open-book leader, or a guarded-vault leader? Let's describe each of these:

Open book. This leader is fully open with her people. She has nothing to hide and is open about the challenges and difficulties she faces. She shares her feelings appropriately and encourages her people to do the same. She inspires people because of who she is and builds a strong trust relationship with her team. She cares about the people in her charge and wants them to feel like they can speak to her about anything. She is also able to make firm and unpopular decisions, and have difficult conversations, knowing that the trust that has been built will convince her people that her motives are still good.

Guarded vault. This is a leader who has been taught that she needs to be aloof from her team, that keeping people on their toes and not letting them know everything that is going on is a strong way to lead. She will hear the problems that people have but will not share her own. She believes that a leader is a strong, impenetrable person who is never rattled. Her people must simply trust her because she is the leader. She isn't necessarily better at making difficult decisions, and may even struggle more with them, but cannot really talk about them to others. She doesn't show any weaknesses, because she feels her team will not trust her anymore.

The guarded-vault leader immediately has a disadvantage. While her people may *say* they trust her, they really can't, because they don't know what's going on within her mind. Decisions may come across as inconsistent because the details aren't shared, and this creates further distrust. The guarded-vault leader may well have all the best intentions and interests of her people at heart, but if her people don't know that, and don't feel that, then it's irrelevant. There is no connection.

Exactly what makes someone a guarded-vault leader is probably beyond the scope of this book. They may be introverted, insecure, not trusting of their team, simply not interested, or the company culture may not tolerate perceived weakness. Whatever the reason, all things being equal, such a leader will hamper the influence they have on their team.

Being an open book has always been my natural default. I remember an incident when I first started working. Some recent traumatic personal events had been dealt with, and I had taken a break and was visiting my parents. I was sitting on the floor in the lounge, reading, and out of the blue my dad said, "You can't handle stress very well."

"Why do you say that?" I asked, perplexed at the sudden comment.

"Because you tell people about your problems," he answered.

I still smile when I think of that conversation, because the precise reason why I feel I do handle stress well, is the reason he feels I can't cope—being open and honest with others about how I feel. I didn't engage in the debate, not because I was angry, but because my dad had grown up to believe in stony, stoic silence. "Wear red, so they can't see you bleed" was the school he had attended, and I wasn't going to dent those beliefs.

Many leaders still believe old examples that encourage leaders to be aloof and mysterious, despite the fact that many modern leadership authors say the exact opposite. In *Five dysfunctions of a team*, Patrick Lencioni encourages leaders to allow their teams to see them sweat. John Maxwell is famous for saying, *"People don't care how much you know until they know how much you care"*, and Simon Sinek's talks encourage authentic connections with people. It is unnecessary to keep your people "on their toes" or "off balance" to get them to work at their best. In *Healing from*

Hidden Abuse, Shannon Thomas[19], a social worker who deals with survivors of psychological abuse, says this:

> *"Some toxic people will actually say out loud that they like keeping people off balance. If someone tells you that, run. It is a huge red flag that you are talking to a psychological manipulator."*

Yesterday's picture of a hero has become today's picture of a potential psychopath.

How do you react when you need to become vulnerable? How approachable are you really? Why not ask your team to rate you on a scale of 1-10? The results may just inspire you to take a step that takes your leadership to the next level.

YOUR TURN

1. Are you authentic and approachable, or closed off?

   _____

   _____

   _____

   _____

   _____

2. How approachable and authentic does your team think you are? Have you asked them?

   _____

   _____

   _____

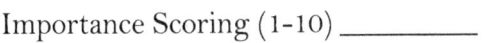

Importance Scoring (1-10) _____

Freedom: Manipulate or Emancipate?

All of us have the ability to manipulate others, and we all have been manipulated in some way or another. Sometimes it is part of a game or a negotiation, other times it is abusive, and in extreme cases it is downright evil. Lately, there are copious reports coming to the fore of abusive behaviors in governments around the world—rape and sexual abuse allegations against prominent people, as well as simple, next-door type of people. It's easy to wonder whether there are any "normal" people left in the world. Then we might also have to ask whether people have perhaps just become fed up and are more open to speaking up against abuses that have been around forever.

Note that I use manipulate and abuse interchangeably, because to me they are the same basic act. You can be manipulated against your will in a relatively harmless interaction, like a pushy sales call, or you can be horribly abused by a psychopath in a way that leaves permanent scars. Both are acts of manipulation, designed to get you to do something against your will, where you lose, and the other person—who does not care about your best interests—wins.

I call this the "Freedom" decision, because manipulation always robs a person of their freedom to act. I have encountered this in many forms in my life, and in some cases I was even doing the manipulating. As I have mentioned before, I have a strong need to preserve my freedom to act, and manipulation by another goes completely against that. If I sense my freedom is in jeopardy, I react strongly. People generally don't get manipulated in an enjoyable way. The abuser takes their victims' goodwill for granted or simply abuses it, with absolutely no interest in their well-being.

But why am I talking about abuse and manipulation as a decision point in leadership? Because you will have to decide, time and time again, whether you will manipulate someone to get your way, or whether you will emancipate them to discover their own way. You will undoubtedly also have to decide whether you will allow yourself to be manipulated by someone else, irrespective of cost.

The better way is, of course, to emancipate. This means to allow people the space to make their own decisions, to work with them in order to find appropriate solutions or, in some cases, to explain why the current solution has to be followed. Even in the latter case people should be free to do something different—and face the consequences—but it isn't a win-lose battle. The motivation behind

> *"The motivation behind emancipation is to value the other person, to develop them and to do what is best for them, within the reasonable context of the situation."*

emancipation is to value the other person, to develop them and to do what is best for them within the reasonable context of the situation. In order to emancipate, the leader needs to understand boundaries and to be firm in setting them, while allowing the follower to move freely within those boundaries or choose to disengage. The highest level of emancipation is to grow followers into leaders themselves. My ultimate example of emancipation is how Christ dealt with His followers—there was never any forcing, coercing or coaxing. He would simply say something like it is, and then leave His followers to make up their own minds, respecting their decision. He certainly wasn't wishy-washy. He had firm boundaries and disciplines, but didn't force anything on people. He always gave them the choice—both for decisions and consequences—and that is what true emancipation is in this context.

In this section, I will describe a few incidents in my life that required a "Freedom" decision, because this decision takes many forms. I believe it is also important to understand the games that often get played, and to recognize them when they happen. They often aren't immediately obvious, mostly because we are oblivious to the motives behind the games.

I CAN BE MANIPULATIVE

If asked whether we can be abusive, we would mostly deny it vehemently, but that isn't always true. At least, it wasn't in my case. My very first job after leaving the army was at Armscor, a weapons manufacturer for the South African

Defense Force. I worked with a great bunch of guys, but the work could be a little convoluted. Since the projects were classified, getting information was done in an obtuse way, since asking international agencies for certain things directly would immediately divulge the type of weapon we were working on. This led to a culture, at least within me, that the end justified the means, and doing what was needed to get the job done was kind of exciting. After all, I was only 23 years old.

One day, my boss called me into his office for a chat. He was an extremely kind person, and never wanted to ruffle feathers. His message to me went as follows: "Dieter, I know that in your job you sometimes need to cross a few lines in order to get the information we require. You have proven that you are quite skilled at that. However, you need to understand it doesn't work like that in here. So, I would like to know from you, how on earth you managed to get my secretary to do your typing as a higher priority than mine!" He laughed as he said it, and it was quite amusing, but his message was clear. I realized that even "minor" manipulation had consequences.

It didn't feel good.

MANIPULATION AS A TACTIC

Fast forward about 15 years and I was the HR director of ABC Manufacturing*. The industry was going through a tough time with global sourcing and world-wide price reductions. As part of our survival strategy we had to retrench a number of people, and it was my job to negotiate the retrenchments with the trade union. The particular union was a militant one that had a political agenda, and the negotiations were not going to be easy. Once the negotiations started, the manipulation games began. I was told that the union officials were trained in these tactics, which are designed to get the opposition off-course and angry, and then—in typical abuser style—focus on *your* behavior and completely ignore their part in instigating it. It started with the small things, such as constantly being late for meetings, like two hours late. Then, in those meetings, they would sit slouched in their chairs, cap drawn over the eyes, seemingly asleep. When you have come prepared with all the reasons, ready for a mature and adult negotiation, this riles you. But to get riled is to lose, because the retrenchment process stops if the union walks away, and you need the retrenchment process to continue. The union cannot be disregarded, so they manipulate with their presence as the prize.

They also employed a sly tactic known as "intermittent reinforcement". This is well-described by Shannon Thomas[19] in *Healing from Hidden Abuse.* It effectively means that abusers, or manipulators, don't abuse every day. As humans, we expect the best from others. The good days give us a high and then we get dumped into the depths again, never realizing that this is exactly the desired intent of the manipulator. So the manipulator will treat you surprisingly well, and just as you think you're getting somewhere, they will hit you with an argument out of left field. This sets up an emotional response in the person being manipulated. In the case of the union, we might have had a meeting where great progress had seemingly been made, and I would leave the meeting in very high spirits, reporting back to the board on this amazing progress. A day or two later I would get a fax from the union, with pages and pages of incorrect and insulting allegations that had to be responded to—and negating all the (false) progress that had been made. I know for a fact that this was a tactic because the faxes always came on a Friday afternoon, or the Thursday before the Easter long weekend, or at a time where I was starting to look forward to some downtime and I foolishly lowered my guard. Initially, it evoked hot anger in me, but I learnt to just leave it until I was calm and then deal with my formal response on the weekend.

The impact of a "little" tactic like this is not trivial. The telephone to which the fax machine was attached had a particular, and quite rare, ringtone. Even now, 15 years after these negotiations, when I happen to hear that ringtone somewhere, I go cold. It's quirky and makes for a funny story, but the underlying damage that can be done by a seriously abusive individual is clear. And not at all funny.

In response to the union tactics, I had to get into the ring myself. For example, discussions with union officials behind the scenes, playing one school of thought off against another— causing internal strife—all in order to get them to sign off on an agreement. It got even more petty. Because they came late to the meetings and dragged them on, I didn't want them to be too comfortable. So, before the meeting started, hoping that it would shorten the meeting, I would open the shades and position myself with my back to windows so they would be staring into bright light.

I had no choice but to hang in there and play the game until the end. And after nine months of negotiating, the union signed off on an agreement that I had proposed right from the beginning. The labor lawyer called it a success, since it was an agreement that was quite novel. However, I felt it had been nine months of wasted time, time where I, on behalf of the employer, had to defend the workers against their own union. And I had had to resort to tactics that I abhorred. I hated every minute of that negotiation experience, and while it had taught me a great deal, the emotional toll had been significant, probably because I had to work in a way that went against my core. A month later, I resigned from that job, partly as a result of this experience.

MANIPULATION AND THE SURVIVOR GAME

We all know this one. At school someone might say, "I won't be your friend unless..." and so you either get manipulated or tell the person to be on their way. However, this can happen all through life, in social settings, at home, or in the workplace. When I was appointed to the board of a company, two of the directors invited me for lunch and a chat. They explained that they were opposed to some of the MD's ideas and wanted to know if they could count on me to follow their lead and join their "team". Presumably that meant I would also get support from them when needed. I responded by saying that they could count on me to do my job to the best of my abilities, and that I didn't need to join a team to do that. Each decision and circumstance would be treated on its own merits.

Lunch ended soon after that.

CLOSE CONTACT MANIPULATION

If you've ever been in the crosshairs of a serial manipulator or abuser, you will know how difficult it is to identify and deal with such people. You will not be able to beat them at their own game. You will not be able to independently expose them without a massive fight, and with a small prospect of success. The reason is that they are manipulators, and you are not, and unless you have CCTV cameras everywhere, no one would believe what you say. They could be in any form, a manager, a team member, an in-law, a spouse, a friend, a parent or a child.

In the workplace they can make your life hell, just because it is fun for them. You can try and stick it out, but then you are in their territory—engagement. Your "Freedom" decision point is difficult because it has career implications. In many cases, other people will be completely unaware that this kind of manipulation is going on. There are two ways in which you can deal with the situation, either leave the company or minimize contact and interaction with the individual. Neither one is a win, but from personal experience a start-over is way more appealing than a long-term, slow poisoning. It *will* affect you. But if you have to stay, you will have to put firm boundaries in place and defend them consistently. You will also have to learn not to react, and at the same time, not internalize. It is possible, but it will be a tough road. Recently, I read this quote:

> *"When we make the intolerable tolerable, we sow the seeds of our own future disaster."*

This is exactly what happens gradually with long-term manipulation—we begin to tolerate it and eventually there are only losers—ourselves, as well as the people we might have had a positive impact on, if only we hadn't been so distracted with the manipulator. And the manipulator will not care.

Manipulation tactics are often used in business, from subtle to overt. Sometimes these tactics are even encouraged in order to get the job done. It is up to you to decide whether manipulation will be part of your leadership style—either by doing it, or by tolerating it.

Have you faced any "Freedom" decision points? Did you decide to manipulate or emancipate? Or did you decide to allow yourself to be manipulated or did you demand emancipation? How familiar are you with the games that are played?

YOUR TURN

1. Will you engage in manipulation tactics?

_____

_____

_____

_____

2. How will you respond when someone attempts to manipulate you or your team?

_____

_____

_____

_____

_____

_____

3. How might your frame of reference affect your view?

_____

_____

_____

_____

Importance Scoring (1-10) _____

Ego: Conviction or Stubbornness?

There is a fine line between sticking to convictions and just being plain stubborn. I've been accused of being very stubborn at times, and I could always justify it by saying that I'm sticking to certain convictions. But was that really so? If I take a good, honest look at those occasions, they fall into one of two categories, namely doing something because I *believe it is the right thing to do* and doing something because I *want to do it my way*. They sound different, they feel different, and they are different.

Conviction. When you are convinced that a particular course of action is the correct way to go, and you have heard all the pro's and con's and weighed up the alternatives the best you can, then you act on that conviction. The motive behind this is not to be right, but to do what's best for the particular situation in your family or organization. You have a strong sense that doing something else would be a mistake. It does not necessarily guarantee that the decision is the correct one, but your motive for making it, is.

Stubbornness. When you want to follow a course of action, not only because you may believe it is right, but also because you have a need to have it done *your* way. When other alternatives present themselves, you dismiss them because you want it done the way you have already decided. You have a strong sense that doing something else would mean you have lost. It does not necessarily mean that your way is wrong, but your motive for insisting on it, is.

"Do you have a need to be right, or do you have a need for the decision to be the correct one?"

These two approaches are very similar, and yet the energy and the emotions are completely different. When you are faced with this, you are looking at an "Ego" decision. Do you have a need to be right, or do you have a need for the decision to be the correct one? It's a very grey area, but check your emotions. In extreme cases, sticking to stubborn guns becomes counter-productive, and actually starts hurting the organization (or your family). The main difference between the two approaches is humility, and that is why this is the "Ego" decision.

A small boutique consulting company, triVector, specializes in business process management consulting. The CEO, Dina Jacobs, is a talented professional, both technically and in the leadership of the business. My role in the business was as the regional manager for the Western Cape region. I was also part of the exco and a minor shareholder.

For triVector, the Western Cape became a "region" when we formally started managing it. That became my job and I relocated from Johannesburg. The pace is slower, and the sales cycles are different, and people first want to get to know each other properly before doing business together. This is in stark contrast to Johannesburg where the aim is to do business, and so things move on a bit faster. After I had been there a number of months, and the results were slow in coming, Dina asked what we needed to change to get the business going. I made a very insistent case for not changing anything, because we were doing the right things, and the results would follow. I was absolutely convinced there was no better way forward in that situation. Eventually, Dina asked when we would see results and on instinct, I gave a date about six months down the line, and she relented. Six months later, the results came in and stayed there. I did not feel vindicated or relieved. I felt good about us having stuck to what works and allowed the process to unfold. It was a success for the company. This was an example of conviction—it was calm, peaceful and just felt right.

Not all my calls in that position were based on conviction, though. While Dina and I got on well, and still do, we often had passionate debates because we had different ways of doing things. As a result, the Western Cape office culture was different to the Johannesburg culture. Neither one was better than the other, but the fact that the culture was so diverse, in retrospect, was a failing on my part. It's not in the best interests of the company to have a culture clash, and as the junior partner in this instance, I ought to have aligned myself with the head office more. But I was stubborn. It was my area and I wanted to do it in my way. My motive for having things done in my way was not for the company, but for myself, and the emotions around this aspect were not calm and peaceful, but rather a tug-o-war for territory. My choice, when faced with the "Ego" decision in this case, was stubbornness.

This may be a normal situation in companies with regional offices, and our politics really weren't very bad at all, but in retrospect, I believe I could have done better by tempering my stubbornness. We all have limited energy and limited time, and to waste them on these kinds of political debates is not effective. You may also ask what to do in the case where the head office isn't being run well? Go back to the "Ego" question—is it conviction, *true* conviction, or stubbornness? In the case of triVector, I cannot claim for a second that the head office wasn't being run well—on the contrary. My only reason for wanting to do things my way was because it would be more comfortable for me. However, had the head office been dysfunctional, I would then have worked to make my regional office as functional as possible within those boundaries.

In my leadership coaching work, I have come across this regional "squaring off" in a number of companies I have worked with. It is not healthy, takes up way too much of a CEO's time to deal with, and takes the focus off doing the main function, namely serving the customer and the company's vision. In every case, when I have spoken with the individuals in the problematic regions, the attitude from the regional manager has been that it's their area and they want to do it their way. It does not mean that a regional manager cannot have different habits within agreed boundaries, but you cannot have a regional office undermining the efforts of a *functioning* head office. The best way forward is to see whether both "ways" can be aligned, and if not, the regional manager has to adopt the head office's way, and if they can't, they should move. They have to make an "Ego" decision.

Can you identify times when you have been convinced and times when you have been stubborn? How did they feel different? If you were going to face them again, how would you handle them now? How would you back away from a purely stubborn stance?

YOUR TURN

1. Do you mostly act out of conviction or out of stubbornness?

_____

_____

_____

2. How do they feel different?

_____

_____

_____

_____

_____

3. What would it mean for you to follow someone else's direction?

_____

_____

_____

_____

Importance Scoring (1-10) _____

Pressure: Popular or Principle?

A point will come where you will be under pressure to decide to do what is *popular*, or to decide to do what is *right*. This decision also comes in many forms during various times in our lives, from peer pressure at school, to pressure from kids while parenting, and on into later years as well. Sometimes the implications are inconsequential, and other times they mark a key decision point in your life or career.

I am inspired by people who stick to principles but are also flexible enough to let the principle go if the issue and example are inconsequential. An example of the latter was when I was dealing with my mom's estate. The court had decided that her will was invalid for what I thought was a stupid reason, namely a smudge on the ink, which offended me on quite a deep

> *"A point will come where you will be under pressure to decide to do what is popular, or to decide to do what is right."*

level, especially given that we had made every effort to do things completely by the book. The result was that her estate would be handled slightly differently, but that the outcome would be much the same. If I just agreed to the court's decision, we could have it wrapped up in a short time. My executor advised that we could fight the court's decision, but that it would potentially extend the process by years. The obvious move here is not to stand on principle, but to opt for expediency.

There is a saying that goes like this:

> *"If you don't stand for something, you will fall for anything."*

A good way to tell what you stand for, is to take note of the "Pressure" decisions that come your way. Nelson Mandela stood against the popular decision to remove the Springbok emblem from South African rugby in order to stand for unifying the country. This is nicely shown in the movie[20] of the 1995 Rugby World Cup, *Invictus*. Abraham

Lincoln stood against the South in order to abolish slavery, and seeing it through to the end, at the risk of being charged with treason. Thus, the people who inspire us, do so because they stand for something. It stands to reason, therefore, that the people we lead will be inspired by us if we stand for something, rather than being nice guys who go with the flow.

One of my most memorable "Pressure" decisions happened when I was in charge of services in a foundry. I was called into the boardroom where I was met by my junior metallurgist, the sales director, the MD, the production director, the projects director, the foundry manager, and the design engineer, Hein. A failure had occurred at one of our clients' testing centers, and the client wanted to send a delegation to audit our processes. While the failure wasn't safety critical, it still wasn't ideal. What I wasn't aware of, though, was that the potential for the failure had already been discovered internally, but one of the directors had worked with my junior metallurgist to present statistically reasonable results and send the product anyway. This was not the way we normally ran the business.

Hein and I were being asked to participate in giving the clients a tour through the factory, showing them all the good stuff we did, and all the reports we had on their particular product. We were to do this knowing full well that we had hidden some potentially incriminating data. Hein, an extremely principled individual, flatly refused and asked to be excused from the meeting. He left, and I sat on the one end of the table, most of the board on the other, with the metallurgist nervously looking at me. The argument went back and forth and I asked whether there wasn't a way we could introduce the data, or come clean, or do something that would allow us to move forward without digging ourselves into a deeper hole. Eventually the debate ended. The board was sure of their stance, and the MD asked me, "Well, are you with us or against us?"

This was a company where I was building my career, and the consequences of going against them could be severe. However, if I agreed, I was going against my own principles. And the metallurgist, who reported to me, was looking to me to exonerate his involvement.

This was a classic "Pressure" decision point.

Eventually, I said that I could not be part of it and if the client came for a tour, they should stay away from me. I got up and walked out, shaking nervously and convinced I would be fired for my decision. Even so, I was extremely glad to have made it. I also spoke with the metallurgist afterwards and we had no issues with each other. As it turned out, I wasn't fired. I was promoted about six months later. The client also didn't come for a tour.

The story does not end there.

The pressure I felt in that meeting was immense. I cannot take credit here for having made that decision simply on my own. I had witnessed Hein standing up to the board and declaring, without compromise, that this was wrong. He had left the meeting because he did not want to be convinced otherwise. If I had not had that example of standing for principle, it's quite possible that I would have folded and given in—following the popular path instead of the principled one. I am forever grateful for Hein's example.

This story describes an imperative decision point for me, because it reminds me of two things. The first is obviously the fact that sometimes we will have to stand up for our convictions, and that can be tough and daunting. The second point, however, is even more important: the power of a role model to build you up or tear you down.

I'm under no illusion—if different people had been in that room, I might have decided differently, but a good role model provided the input I needed to make a decision that I could be proud of—and refer back to—for the rest of my life. It's not my decision that inspires me, it is Hein's.

> *"A good role model provided the input I needed to make a decision that I could be proud of, and refer back to, for the rest of my life."*

When I asked Hein if I could include this story in my book, he initially did not want to be named in any way, because he didn't deserve the credit, God did. I felt that the story provided a testimony to what God had done in his life, and so we agreed to put it in.

What pressure decisions have you faced, or are anticipating facing? What role models do you have in your life from whom you can ask advice? What will you do?

YOUR TURN

1. Under what circumstances would you make a principle decision?

_____

_____

_____

_____

_____

_____

_____

2. Who would you be a role model for?

_____

_____

_____

_____

Importance Scoring (1-10) _____

Criticism: Energizing or Discouraging?

If you are a leader, you will be criticized. If you are a leader who has a style that's different from the company culture, you will be *strongly* criticized. If you are a leader who questions the status quo, you will be *vehemently* criticized. But criticism *will* come your way. It is inevitable. Even if you are getting good results, you will still get criticized.

The question is not *whether* you will be criticized, it is deciding how to deal with the criticism that gets levelled at you. Will you allow it to get you down, or will it inspire you to achieve more?

> *"Criticism may not be agreeable, but it is necessary. It fulfils the same function as pain in the human body. It calls attention to an unhealthy state of things."*
> – Winston Churchill

> *"I have benefitted greatly from criticism, and at no time have I suffered a lack thereof."* –
> Winston Churchill

> *"Criticism is easy; achievement is difficult."*
> – Winston Churchill

> *"If you can't tolerate critics, don't do anything new or interesting."* – Jeff
> Bezos

The "Criticism" decision point is intentional. When criticized, the initial reaction is to retaliate in some way, but as leaders we have to develop a skin that is both thick and wise. We must decide that we will take any and all criticism that is levelled against us, and judge it to see whether it is helpful or not. We judge criticism by the following points:

Who is doing the criticizing? There are certain people in our lives whose opinions matter more to us than others'. In some cases this is warranted, like a friend or mentor who generally gives very good advice. Other times it is destructive, like seeking approval from someone who doesn't have your best interests at heart. Does the critic have experience in the topic they are commenting on or not? If the opinion comes from a source that we do not deem credible, the criticism could be discarded. Even so, it is always worth investigating whether a comment has some merit.

What are they saying? Some criticisms are constructive, while other criticisms are purely an alternative opinion, and some are just a downright attack. We must judge whether the criticism we receive is helpful to improve what we are attempting to achieve, or whether it detracts from the objective. If the criticism is a personal attack, then we have to ask what the critic's motives are.

Why are they saying it? Some people may criticize because they genuinely feel that your action or opinion is wrong and not in the best interests of the group you are serving. In other cases, people are attempting to discredit you personally in favor of pushing their own agendas. This sadly seems to be case in most political arguments. The most unthinking critic of all will criticize everything you say, irrespective of what it is, simply because you belong to another group or they want to get even for some perceived injustice, or they feel threatened by you. The motive behind criticism is a strong indicator of how seriously, and in what context, to take the criticism.

How often is it said? Irrespective of the person, the subject or the motive, if you hear the same comment coming at you multiple times from multiple sources, then you need to take note. An MD I used to report to, used to say, "If one person says you are drunk all the time, you can laugh it off. But if ten people say the same thing, you need help." This is an interesting one, because it's easy to miss if we merely judge each criticizing incident one at a time. For the record, my MD was being hypothetical and wasn't referring to anyone's drinking problem in particular.

> *"Criticism, though unpleasant, is necessary for your growth."*

Criticism, though unpleasant, is necessary for your growth. You have to choose, intentionally choose, to accept criticism from people, even those who deeply offend you. Note that accepting the criticism does not mean you agree with it. Accept it as a comment to be evaluated and judged, and then decide whether it needs to be acted upon.

I have had various types of criticisms. I have had criticism of ideas and actions that I have welcomed and have included in forming better solutions. This helped me to become teachable, and I see this as a necessary part of leading. I have had criticism that has hurt deeply, but on investigation and reflection, found it to be accurate and had to make amends (and amendments). I have also had criticism that was plain stupid, like a director of a company telling me, "You'll never get anywhere in this company because you don't swear enough, and you don't walk fast enough." I made it onto the board of directors.

In my leadership journey, I have received heaps of praise and hills of criticism. You probably have too. The praise is easy to deal with, but you also have to take valid criticism seriously. You don't grow when things are always going right, because all you are doing is what you already know. But when things go wrong, and criticism abounds, you need to take stock, use the data, and plan to move forward. Therefore, the criticism becomes an energizer—a necessary energizer—to growth and improvement.

Accept that criticism is a sign that you are in fact doing something worthwhile. If you were sitting on the stands, simply watching life, there would be no criticism.

I love this famous quote from Theodore Roosevelt, called *"The Man in the Arena"*.

> *"It is not the critic who counts; not the man who points out how the strong man stumbles, or where the doer of deeds could have done them better. The credit belongs to the man who is actually in the arena, whose face is marred by dust and sweat and blood; who strives valiantly; who errs, who comes short again and again, because there is no effort without error and shortcoming; but who does actually strive to do the deeds; who knows great enthusiasms, the great devotions; who spends himself in a worthy cause; who at the best knows in the end the triumph of high achievement, and who at the worst, if he fails, at least fails while daring greatly, so that his place shall never be with those cold and timid souls who neither know victory nor defeat."*

Don't let criticism, no matter how accurate or undeserved, discourage you. Let it energize and grow you. How do you respond to criticism? What emotions come up when you are criticized?

YOUR TURN

1. Does criticism energize or discourage you?

_____

_____

_____

_____

_____

_____

2. When criticism hits a home truth, what do you do?

_____

_____

_____

_____

3. How thoughtful are you when criticizing others?

_____

_____

_____

_____

Importance Scoring (1-10) _____

Intentionality: Growth or Stagnation?

"Do you have a five-year plan?"

This is a question that, for most of my adult life, would cause a spontaneous burst of apathy. I had the attitude that, as long as I worked hard and put in my time, I would end up where I needed to be. Many of my work colleagues and friends felt much the same way. Here and there someone had a five-year plan and goals, and I thought it seemed like a lot of hard work, and then just went with the flow. Hopefully, by reading this, you will stop and make the "Intentionality" decision a lot earlier than I did.

In the subconscious recesses of my mind there probably was some form of target that I was aiming at, based on my beliefs and interests. But it definitely wasn't intentional. That is perhaps why I have made many career changes, always looking for that "thing", but never investigating what the "thing" might actually be. One might say that my searching has been physical trial and error, rather than trying to think things through first. I wasn't really aware that the "Intentionality" decision existed. In the early 2000s I stumbled onto John Maxwell's leadership and teamwork books and applied them to my leadership team in the ABC Manufacturing* foundry. It was an extremely rewarding experience that started a quest into the leadership theme for me, applying it wherever the flow took me.

But in September 2013, at the age of 47, all that changed. I presented a talk on "influence" at an international IT conference, and the response was so positive that I knew I wanted to do more of that. I needed to make some form of change. I started a Google search and very soon discovered the John Maxwell Team, offering certification in leadership coaching. I didn't really know what coaching was, but the rest sounded good, and after having paid my daughter's studies for many years, it was now my turn. I enrolled, not really knowing what to expect, but with an excitement I hadn't felt for years.

Being South African, I felt that there was a lot of American hype around the course, but if John Maxwell was behind it, I believed in it. The JMT ran on world-wide conference calls, and when I had paid my fee, I signed in on the first introductory call. Paul Martinelli, president of the JMT was hosting. He gave the full background, and when it came to Q&A, I was near the front of the line. I asked him whether the course was really that good. His words to me were these: "If you do the work, I *guarantee* that in a year's time you will need a telescope to see how far you've come."

So, I climbed in and did the work. In listening to the various talks, lectures, videos, discussions and group calls, I noticed something fundamentally different between the teaching team and myself. They were intentional about every minute of every day. Either the minute was serving them in some way, or it didn't exist. They literally *spent their time* wisely. I was blowing my time on circumstance. I made the decision to grow, since I

> "Not everyone wants to grow, and therefore your growth means that you can grow apart."

realized that that was actually what I had missed whenever I had reached the stage of being bored in a job. I wasn't growing! To most of you that's obvious. To me it was a revelation. Maybe—in hindsight—it seems self-evident, but a revelation, nonetheless.

I decided to make every minute count as well. I started reading non-fiction books on subjects that interested me, rather than only novels. I tried to have a positive impact on someone every day. I worked hard at the new skills I was learning, and engaged where I could. I got a little obsessed, wanting to make up for lost time. Just a note of caution here: If you make the "Intentionality" decision to grow when it's completely unfamiliar to you and all your friends, you don't just upset the apple cart, you blow it to smithereens! Your interests and hobbies change, your language changes, your way of interacting changes, and many life-long parts of your life get rattled. I say this, not to avoid the decision, but to make you aware that un-tempered enthusiasm when acting on this decision could be painful. Not everyone wants to grow, and therefore your growth means that you can grow apart.

My initial burst of enthusiasm has been followed by a more stable growth, eventually resulting in a depth that has undoubtedly changed my character. I feel it in the contentment that I have in what is around me, while at the same time working to achieve a greater impact. I also leave intentional time to relax and sometimes just do nothing.

I can confirm that Paul was right. After a year, I couldn't believe how far I had mentally moved, and now, after seven years of growth—and counting—the Hubble space telescope wouldn't be able to find my starting point. I will always be grateful to the JMT teaching team and colleagues for continually providing that input.

I still don't have a five-year plan, in the sense that it is completely mapped out and cast in stone. What I do have, are five-year goals and direction. The steps in how to get there are resolved as I go along, because the goals are mostly bigger than my current abilities, and I don't know how I will achieve them. But, as I learn and as circumstances unfold, new possibilities open up and the next few steps are revealed.

Your Turn

1. Are you growing or stagnating?

_____

_____

_____

2. Do you have five-year goals? If not, try and write some down, why don't you?

_____

_____

_____

_____

_____

_____

_____

_____

3. What would you need to do today to start growing intentionally?

_____

_____

_____

Importance Scoring (1-10) _____

Source: Intuition or Information?

Do you ever use intuition to make decisions? It's that gut feel, which you cannot explain, that prompts you to make certain calls. Often these are game-changing decisions, going against the course of what is reasonable and practical, where the pro's are smothered by con's… and yet the decisions are correct. Our intuition can also be off, leading to gut-feel decisions that cause harm. As a result, decisions are then only made if they can be supported and justified by hard-and-fast, documented evidence. So, even if it goes wrong, the evidence puts us in the clear. As the old saying goes, *"No-one ever got fired for hiring IBM."*

Good leaders use intuition. It's important to realize that even the information we have is flawed—and incomplete. It's only the information we have at our disposal *at that point in time*, not *all* the information. The additional, after-the-fact information may reveal something else. But, unfortunately, we don't have it yet, and a call still needs to be made. True leadership failure does not lie in making a wrong decision, it lies in not making a decision when one is required. There are a few things to take into account about decisions in general.

Multiple right ways. When we were at school, decisions were simple. Should we study for the exam or should we loaf and watch TV? Here, there is an obvious right decision and an obvious wrong one. But life seldomly throws us those "cut the blue wire or the red wire" decisions. As you can see when you look at the illustration on the cover of this book, most of our big decisions have multiple options with multiple outcomes. Ultimately, we need to think through the facts and make our best call.

> "True leadership failure does not lie in making a wrong decision, it lies in not making a decision when one is required."

Decisions are followed by action. The decision itself doesn't define right or wrong. Once we make a decision on a course of action, we take action and move forward. The speed, competence, enthusiasm and drive behind the action often determine whether the outcome is successful. Or to put it another way, we make a decision, and then make it right.

We can't make a decision using hindsight. Once the outcome of a decision becomes clear—because all the facts emerge—people take it upon themselves to become expert analysts on the "coulda, shoulda and woulda" of any outcome. But the same people often wouldn't have had the stomach to make a call based on the information available at the time the call was required. Even the best call will be open to harsh criticism by others once more facts become clear and hindsight is available. But that is the point—hindsight is not available at the time of making the decision. This is obvious, but conveniently forgotten by critics. When you are in a leadership position, expect to be criticized even for good decisions, and realize that you were fortunate if it was a perfect outcome.

Using intuition is one of the magic weapons a leader has. It goes further than simply making decisions—it informs as well. It's the skill to pick up what's going on around you and making calls that are not obvious. Leaders are in the people business, and looking at charts and reports only gives you some of the information, and can only inform on what has already happened. However, moving around the office or factory, feeling the "vibe" and getting a sense of morale will tell you more about what the report will look like tomorrow. This is working on the "cause" end of the law of cause and effect, which I described earlier. Yesterday's report can't change, but tomorrow's is a whole new canvas. Intuition is often hard to explain, and therefore people may shy away from it, but I believe it to be an invaluable part of leaders' skills and allows them to tap into knowledge that they don't know they have. We just have to be open to use it, even if we can't explain it. Using this intuition can even be a matter of life and death, as I'll describe later.

People are often described as "intuitive", or we might tell ourselves we are "not intuitive". This is wrong thinking. I believe intuition is available to everyone who desires to use it. I believe the following about intuition.

Everyone is intuitive in their area of strength. I remember an occasion where I had just left a 24-hour production environment after having been there for eight years. We ran three shifts of eight hours each, and the various calculations of manpower, how many people were needed for a task, and so forth, was a daily function. In the new role at a different company, which was unfamiliar with this, someone asked how many people would be required for a certain task if we worked around the clock. Within seconds I had worked it out in my head and could give an accurate answer. The other members around the table just looked at me and asked, "How did you do that?"

"I don't know. I just did," I answered. This is a tell-tale sign of intuition based on an area of strength. For the record, now, years after having left that environment, I would not be able to do that calculation at all. I would have to think it through first and figure it out. Not practicing, even in an area of strength, means that you lose the intuition.

Intuition, like a muscle, can be honed and strengthened. In 1994 I did a day-long program of psychometric tests. At that stage I was nearing 30—young and full of all the answers. I was very black-and-white in my thinking. My Myers-Briggs profile declared that I was an ESTP, and on the Sensing-Intuitive (S-N) axis, I was off the charts on "S". The psychologist doing the tests reported that I was unable to make decisions unless I had all the facts, I was not intuitive, and that this would limit my career. My boss at the time, also a friend, was a strong "N", or intuitive, and he told me that he would do better than I would in life because he was intuitive. Whether the advice was accurate or flawed is not relevant, but this whole situation annoyed me, and I purposely started making decisions when I knew I didn't have all the facts, but enough to make decent calls. Over time I became better at it, and some years later, I was described by one of my colleagues as a person who "could foresee things". Some twenty years later, I am very comfortable in the grey areas of life, and I am suspicious of a black-and-white opinion. It would be interesting to see what a Myers-Briggs test would say now!

Intuition can come from outside ourselves. Here you may feel that the discussion is getting weird, but stay with it. There is much we don't know about the subconscious mind, but we do know that it is more powerful than the conscious, rational mind. Some estimates I have seen say about sixty times more, but it depends on what and how it's measured. The subconscious gathers data all the time—using all the senses and emotions—and stores and catalogues everything. The rational mind won't even be aware of most of this data, but it does exist. The subconscious works at a phenomenal speed, and thoughts and answers can come quickly. I believe the subconscious can also pick up on "thoughts" that are outside of ourselves, almost like a radio picks up stations, and if a thought is powerful enough it may leave a sense of something for us to follow up on. I like to call them "pings", for want of a better word. Personally, in my faith journey I have come to understand the term "the voice of

God" only since I began to perceive and accept how the subconscious operates.

But let me give you an example that, to this day, is very vivid. I was managing the ABC Manufacturing* foundry, and I was walking in the plant. The foundry was made up of four head-height platforms, each accommodating eight low-pressure die-casting machines. Each machine is a bit like a massive steel sandwich, with two steel platens, measuring about 1.5 m by 1.5 m by 30 cm thick, with a die between the two platens. The machines open by moving the top platen upwards to open the die. As I was walking towards the office block near the first platform, I noticed an unattended gas burner, with flames coming out of it. It wasn't a safe practice, but it was not an uncommon thing— in a foundry, burners are everywhere and used for various things. But, somehow, this one sent a *ping* to my brain. Normally, when I saw something like that, I would go to the relevant platform manager and tell him about it so that he could deal with it. This was intentional, because I did not want to interfere with their authority unless there was an immediate safety concern. But even as I walked towards the manager's office, the *ping* hit me again. I had to find out about that burner. I walked up to the first machine, which happened to be open. The operator, Freddy*, was busy attending to a die in the open machine. I asked why the burner was unattended. He couldn't hear me, so he moved out from between the platens onto a catwalk so that he could hear me. In that moment, the hydraulic shaft that had held the machine open, snapped, and the top platen came crashing down where he had been standing only moments before. He would not only have been killed, there would have been various body parts lying around. There are many ways to try and explain this, but the bottom line is that if I hadn't heeded those multiple *pings*, Freddy would be dead. Learning how to recognize when intangible and unexplained feelings or compulsions are trying to guide us, is a skill we can all learn.

INTUITION AND BUSINESS

Colin Powell[21] has 13 rules for leadership, summarized in *It Worked for Me: In Life and Leadership*. Rule number six states:

> **"Don't let adverse facts stand in the way of a good decision.** *Superior leadership is often a matter of superb instinct. Often, the factual analysis alone will indicate the right choice. More often, your judgment will be needed to select from the best courses of action."*

This re-iterates that there are multiple courses of action, and we must use all of our tools, including gut feel, to make decisions that are often not supported by others. This may not be because of information available, but individuals' differing frames of reference, visions, and ambitions. If the company owner has a vision, he will make decisions in line with that vision and his gut feel, even if the information doesn't support it.

Francois de Kock is the MD of Greenhouse Technologies, which supplies plastic sheeting, irrigation systems and growth media to the agricultural sector.

Francois has been a coaching client of mine for several years. He described a pivotal gut-feel decision, which he had made many years prior, that had established his company.

He had started the company to supply bits and pieces to the flower industry, firstly working from home, and later opening an office in the Johannesburg flower market building. He wanted to build a big company that would have longevity, and where many people would find employment in a family-type atmosphere. In 2007 his turnover was R1.9 million, which was okay for a good lifestyle for his family but didn't shoot the lights out. He needed to grow, and his gut feel was that he needed to get an international partner on board. The financial director was not convinced of the partnership idea, thinking that the company would grow organically. Francois insisted, and they agreed to go and see their bookkeeper to get an opinion. The bookkeeper shared the FD's view that the company was fine, profitable, and didn't need to take on a partner. But Francois had a vision to build more than just any company, and he knew he couldn't do it by himself.

He approached one of his suppliers, Israeli agricultural plastics sheeting producer, Politiv, who was keen to buy a stake in his company, and they sent a contract through. Francois and the FD took the contract to a lawyer who dismissed it as one-sided, and suggested that they rather borrow money to fund the growth. The lawyer felt that having a partner was not what Francois should do. But, again, Francois differed, since debt would put pressure on cashflow, and wouldn't give him the additional mindpower to plan and execute the growth. After raising the lawyer's concern with them, Politiv advised Francois to amend the contract if he wasn't happy with it. Instead, Francois had a business lawyer take a look at it, and together they travelled to Politiv in Israel where a win-win contract was concluded. The equity partnership had been formed. As a result of that partnership, Greenhouse Technologies has grown, and continues to grow to this day. From the R1.9 million in 2007, Greenhouse grew to R12 million in 2008 with the partnership. Today, in 2020, they are aiming at R135 million, with warehouses and branches across South Africa. Politiv continues to play an active role in the company, which employs about 35 people and is continually growing and evolving.

> *"Sometimes you just have to go with your gut. Knowing when it's a good gut instinct takes awareness and practice, and the willingness to take a risk."*

About two years into the partnership, the bookkeeper told Francois that taking on a partner was the correct decision after all, and that he had been wrong. Yet, all the advice and "facts" pointed to not getting a partner.

Sometimes you just have to go with your gut. Knowing when it's a good gut instinct takes awareness and practice, and the willingness to take a risk. Francois has also been wrong in other decisions. One could argue that the partnership could have gone wrong, as partnerships often do. Then I would ask, had it been a less useful partner, would Francois' gut instinct have been the same? We will never know, but what we do know is that being able to make good gut-instinct calls is a necessary part of leadership, and honing this skill will pay way more dividends than, say, another Excel course.

How do you make decisions? How comfortable are you to make decisions when the outcome isn't clear, and not all the information is available? When have you heard that *ping* to do something? Whether you followed it or not, what was the result?

YOUR TURN

1. Do you use intuition to make decisions, or only available facts?

_____

_____

_____

_____

2. Can you think of examples where you did use intuition?

_____

_____

_____

_____

_____

_____

_____

3. What could you do to strengthen your intuition muscle?

_____

_____

_____

_____

_____

Importance Scoring (1-10) _____

Diligence: Wing It or Work at It?

There are leaders who take the job of leading their team seriously. They are intentional about wanting to develop the team and to do a good job of leading. There are other leaders who get into a position and then simply wing it. They do what's needed to get by, but don't grasp the gravity of the position they have been put in. They don't realize the immense privilege of being a mentor to the people they lead. They don't realize that their actions will impact others, and they simply float along, oblivious.

Have you ever been led by a leader who was winging it instead of working at it? Then you will know the frustration of having to follow someone who is not taking their position of leading you, seriously. You will know that this could impact your career. Perhaps you don't know the leader is winging it because they are nice enough and you get on well and just get on with the job. If you aspire to be a good leader, then ask yourself what you are learning from this person. What are they intentionally doing to develop you further or improve your opportunities?

I would like to think that I am a diligent leader, but I also know that this has not always been the case. My first few opportunities at leading were dismal, and it took quite a while before I understood the "Diligence" decision. Looking back at my first opportunity always makes me cringe, but because the bar is set so low, you will definitely be encouraged by the account. So, I have included it here.

I was around 20 years old, final year at varsity, and had been part of a Lutheran church for most of my life. I had taken part in all the usual church things—worship, Sunday school, plays, sports days, cell group, confirmation, youth activities, and the like. It had been a lot of fun and I was part of the crowd, and up until then, responsible for sports and socials. The youth leader, a dear friend to this day, was stepping down and I was voted in as the new youth leader. From the first day, I did not know what I was doing, but I didn't realize it. We did some good things, like a 100 km cycling-tour weekend and a New Year's church camp, but it was all very social and fun. It didn't really dawn on me at all that it was my job to lead the youth. I can't even claim that I wasn't given a job description, because the title said it all—the youth leader! The spiritual aspects of my year in office were sadly lacking, and I remember clearly one Sunday evening when we had a youth service, I started a discussion on a topic and hadn't planned it well enough to actually see it through. There was a bit of awkwardness and the senior pastor took the reins and carried on the debate. Still, I didn't realize my mistake. I just thought that I simply wasn't good at preaching, and that was the end of it. I would stick to my knitting and others could fill in. Except, I should've planned for that—which I didn't, because I was winging it—and didn't even have the awareness to realize it.

The year bumbled along, with little to no spiritual growth for anyone, at least not due to youth activities. But we did do some fun stuff, I kept telling myself. Eventually, the year was up, and a new youth leader was voted in. I was about to go to the army so I wasn't eligible anyway. Usually there was a little ceremony amongst the youth for the outgoing youth leader, but in my case the senior pastor invited us to the parsonage for a social. I thought it was a nice touch, but at that stage I didn't even realize I had failed! Thankfully, in the ensuing years, and in more interactions with youth groups of the churches I had attended, it became obvious to me that I had not served the youth of that Lutheran church well, and I slowly began to understand the privilege of leadership and subsequently became more diligent.

You will see from that example that if you have not led before, you cannot possibly do worse than I did, because by reading this book you are already more aware than I was back then. So, I hope you are encouraged to go out and work at it.

How do you plan your leadership engagements? Would you describe yourself as someone who works at it, or someone who wings it? If the latter, who is being negatively affected?

YOUR TURN

1. When it comes to your leadership, do you wing it, or do you work at it?

_____

_____

_____

2. How is your leadership style impacting your team?

_____

_____

_____

_____

_____

3. What could you do to work at it better?

_____

_____

_____

_____

_____

Importance Scoring (1-10) _____

BEHAVIORAL DECISION POINTS

B ehavioral decision points. These are the decisions that formed the basis of my leadership style and expression. They are in alignment with my foundational beliefs and character traits, but the decision outcome could be dependent on current circumstances. This is *how* I show up.

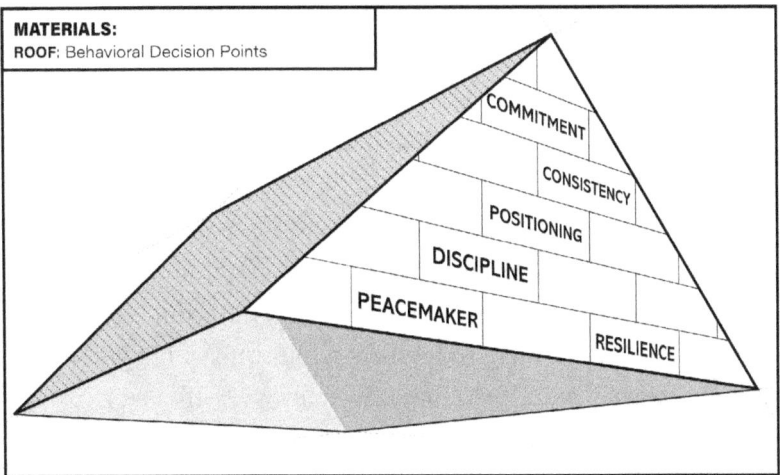

MATERIALS:
ROOF: Behavioral Decision Points

COMMITMENT
CONSISTENCY
POSITIONING
DISCIPLINE
PEACEMAKER
RESILIENCE

The behavioral decision point sections include application examples, because you may choose to behave differently based on circumstances. In these examples I show you alternative situations where your behavior may be different, but still in harmony with your foundational and character decision points.

Commitment: Promise or Possibility?

It may seem odd that this decision is grouped with behavioral ones. After all, keeping your word—keeping a promise—is a fundamental value. It speaks of integrity, trust, character, and so forth. To be honest, when structuring this book, I had the same debate with myself. However, there are times when commitments that have been made might come under pressure. There also seem to be differences of opinion as to what a commitment means. There are also times when commitments had been made where the other party has acted in bad faith. If so, is the commitment still binding?

The "Commitment" decision point investigates how we make commitments, what we see as commitments, and how bound we feel by them. It will also determine how we behave when we have to break a commitment. Do we see a commitment as a firm *promise* that we will keep, or a *possibility* that depends on various factors?

Promise. In this case, you will make a commitment with every intention of keeping it. You will ensure that required resources are in place to fulfill the commitment, and once the commitment is made, you will be aware of it until such time as it is fulfilled. In extreme cases, keeping the commitment can be detrimental to the health of the business or the leader, but is kept anyway. It may seem noble, but becomes detrimental to the team.

Possibility. In this case, a commitment is made knowing that there is a chance that you may not be able to keep it. If you think you are immune to this, then ask yourself when last did you "promise" to take out the trash, take the kids to the movies on Saturday, or even that everything will work out fine. In extreme cases, every commitment is simply a tactic to achieve an aim, and forcing a re-negotiation further down the line.

There is another extreme that exists but is completely senseless. This is where the leader refuses to make any commitments in order to ensure a hypothetical reputation of being someone that keeps their promises. It just isn't possible to be an effective leader, or even individual, if commitments are avoided. People build their hopes and futures on commitments, and if there aren't any, they won't know which way they are heading. A leader who can't give direction, isn't leading.

> *"A leader who can't give direction, isn't leading."*

In the extreme cases of "Promise" or "Possibility", it is true that this is rather a character decision point. But in between the extremes it becomes behavioral, meaning that the circumstances would have an effect on which path is chosen. *How* the path is executed is absolutely a function of character. As a leader, beware—your way of dealing with commitments, especially those made to your team, will be a determining factor of how the team functions, both with other teams and individually between team members. As Stephen Covey[24] put it, breaking a commitment is a major withdrawal from the emotional bank account, and if you do it too often—and don't come through with enough other commitments—your team won't trust you.

If you are, by values and by nature, someone who falls more into the "Promise" camp, then breaking a commitment is a difficult choice. The external consequences, such as reputation, financial penalties, etc., will be less important to you than the internal consequence of seemingly having acted without integrity. If it needs to be done, then the situation is explained to the person or people affected, and care is taken to try and break the commitment in a dignified way. If you are more inclined to the "Possibility" way of thinking, then breaking a commitment would be a clinical view of pro's and con's, justifications and best-case scenarios. You may not even bother to contact people to explain that the commitment would be broken, but rather wait for them to broach the subject.

APPLICATION EXAMPLES

We have all made commitments, kept some, and broken others. No doubt we will have had our reasons and justifications, and depending on your view, these may be more or less justifiable. In order to contrast between the two decision approaches, I will use the comparison of supplier commitments in two company types that represent companies I have been involved with.

In Company A, when a decision is made to purchase a product or service, it is only done if the money is reasonably expected to be in the bank. The company, as a rule, keeps a minimum balance in the account as a risk-mitigation strategy, and when the product or service is delivered, payment is made in the next payment cycle after invoices are received. The company's suppliers are always confident of payment. In the very unlikely case of a default, the directors would be in touch with the supplier, no matter how big or small, to inform and discuss. The attitude is to keep short accounts.

In Company B, when a decision is made to purchase a product or service, it is done because it is needed in order to function. The company may have steady cash inflows and outflows, but whether money will be available for the payment is dependent on customer payments. In order to optimize cashflows, invoices are paid as late as possible, and if there is a cash shortage, suppliers are prioritized and the most important ones for the business are paid first. The smaller or non-critical suppliers are last on the priority list, and if there is an extended cashflow crisis, they just don't get paid. Often, they are not contacted to inform them of this—the company waits until the suppliers ask or beg for payment. Suppliers are expected to understand that this is just business.

It can be argued that both of these are examples of "good" cashflow management. Yet, the impact on the suppliers, and sometimes the employees, is very different.

Company B could say that Company A is lucky to have a bit of a cash pile, but Company A didn't always have the cash pile. They purposely built it up in order to ensure being able to keep their commitments, thereby displaying a "Promise" philosophy.

What would your team's view be of your commitment decisions? When you have to break a commitment to people, how do you go about it? How do the people being affected by the broken commitment respond?

YOUR TURN

1. Do you set yourself up to keep commitments, or do you wait and see how things turn out?

_____

_____

_____

_____

2. How do your team members respond to you when you make a commitment to them? Do they accept it as done, or are they hesitant?

_____

_____

_____

_____

3. Do you need to make any changes?

_____

Importance Scoring (1-10) _____

Resilience: Diesel or Dynamite?

What exactly is "a sense of urgency"? It's a phrase that is used in many interactions, and certainly seems like it's something positive and wanted, and yet, it seems to mean different things to different people. A Google search produced 42 million hits. Leaders simply tell their people to have a sense of urgency and expect that those words will change everyone's behavior for the better. John Kotter defines three different possibilities. The first possibility is complacency, which is the absence of any urgency, and stems from being entirely happy with the status quo. The second is a false sense of urgency which sends people into masses of frenzied activity without being effective in any way. The third is the ideal—a true sense of urgency, where every day is used intentionally to move forward.

> "But as a leader you need to consider how your definition of a sense of urgency, and how you live it out, affect your team."

Unfortunately, in my experience, the "sense of urgency" most often displayed, is the false one. Entrepreneurs especially need to be moving and shaking things up. Probably necessarily so. But as a leader you need to consider how your definition of a sense of urgency—and how you live it out—affect your team. This is where the "Resilience" decision comes into play. Will you be the "Diesel" leader or the "Dynamite" leader? And under what circumstances?

Diesel. Just like a never-say-die tractor on the farm, this style is one of intentionally moving forward, little by little, until the job is done. It does not mean a lack of initiative or a plodder. It means a predictable and reliable approach, resulting in lasting results. In this approach, the leader values the process as well as the results. The pace is determined by when the job reasonably needs to be done.

Dynamite. This style is noticeable and explosive, making things happen and driving themselves and others beyond what they thought possible. Results are important above all else, and the fastest way to get the results is preferred. Demands are sometimes seen as unreasonable, and followers may become discouraged and exhausted.

Both approaches definitely have merit but depending on the circumstances, one may be more effective than the other. Emergency situations often require a dynamite approach to take charge and get things going, whereas longer-term projects would be best managed with a diesel approach. It's clear that these approaches often are a result of the leader's personality, but that's where we have to be careful. We *can* choose, and we owe it to our team to use these approaches effectively.

For the "Dynamite" approach, things have to happen quickly within an allotted time—or faster. If you ask what is urgent, everything is. If you want to know what to focus on, everything needs focus. I had a boss at one stage who drove himself and others very hard. Things all needed to happen immediately, even if they really didn't need to. He would be in the office very early and leave late. In meetings, getting heated about the urgency that was needed to sort out an issue, he would often slam his hand on the table and shout, "We can't just sit around. This is war!" Sense of urgency became a sense of chaos. But unless the business is in imminent risk of failure, or a massive deal is on the line within a short time-frame, or there's a fire, it usually isn't war. As a result, all of us who reported to him were in a constant state of alert, flurrying around to do something, anything, that seemed useful. This is the point of the "Resilience" decision point—what the approach in any given scenario means for the long-term well-being of the team.

Earlier in this book, I spoke about the importance of role models and the immediate elevation of authority that positional power gives a leader. That means that the style and actions of the leader will rub off on the team, and the culture will be set. If you are someone that is driven and always "on", your team will feel they need to be and do the same. If you are the business owner, and your work is your life and highest priority, your team will feel pressured to show the same commitment. You may think this is good news, but it won't be long before your team becomes resentful. After all, they are not owners of the business, and their involvement is governed by a different contract.

Highly-driven leaders should also be aware—and take into account when they draw up schedules or project plans—that every individual has a different capacity for work. This does not make them bad, lazy or ineffective, it simply means that they can't function well without an appropriate amount of rest. In order to show their commitment, however, these employees could end up driving themselves too hard for too long, and burn-out can occur. Real burn-out has long-term consequences. Paul Donders[22], author of *Resilience*, states that only about 20% of people who experience a burn-out will recover fully, 60% bounce back but never fully recover, and 20% get stuck. He further cites a study done in the Netherlands in 2011, where they found that 11% of employees have burn-out symptoms. The economic cost, never mind the individual cost, can become huge.

Burn-out does not occur because people work long and hard on projects that have meaning and make sense. It occurs because of stress and hyperactivity—this sounds very similar to a false sense of urgency! By constantly whipping people up into a frenzy of activity when it isn't warranted, leaders not only harm their business long-term, but also damage the people who are in their care. Colin Powel describes in *It worked for me* that he was always wary of people who are constantly on the go. He calls them "busy bastards" and, where possible, chose not to hire them. The disruptive influence on the team was not justifiable.

Ultimately, the "Resilience" decision point relates directly to a short-term versus long-term picture of the business. As the leader—or possibly the owner—you set the pace and, therefore, also the result. Recently, I saw a leadership case study video where the owner of a business said that he purposely left work at 5pm every day, not to stop working, but to demonstrate to his employees that he did not require them to work long hours if they didn't have to. He carried on working at home if needed. This is a leader who took a long-term view of the "Resilience" decision point, and also understood the impact his example has on his team.

APPLICATION EXAMPLES

If we are leading a team, our example counts, even in the small things. At triVector we had a hard-working CEO. She did not directly demand that people work long hours at all, yet all of us regularly used to receive emails between 7pm and 9pm. The immediate reaction was to drop everything and respond, because the implication was that she needed the information urgently. Initially, this was no problem, but when it happened many evenings, my colleagues and I became weary of it. At our monthly exco meeting, the topic was cautiously raised with Dina that she is perhaps expecting too much of the senior staff. Her answer was enlightening. She explained that her relaxation time was in the evening in front of the TV, and she had the habit of responding to outstanding emails during that time. At no point did she expect from people to respond immediately—she was simply clearing her inbox. The relief in the room was palpable. We had permission to ignore the evening emails if we chose to, and deal with them in the morning. But the message to leaders is clear—your team is always watching and will try and respond in like fashion.

In another example, I once had a strict boss that completely demanded too much—me. In fact, I have the same boss now, but thankfully he's learnt from his mistakes. I hope. I had started my coaching business and had run it full time for just over two years. It was tough going, and contracts and income were sporadic. Many months I didn't know how the bills would get paid and I would frantically do something, anything, to "make things happen". I would accept speaking engagements and marketing opportunities which I knew would not yield any results, but always told myself, "You never know what can happen and who you might meet..." I had transitioned from a busy corporate career to an even busier solo career without missing a beat—and two years later I was like a whirlwind, doing "stuff" and thinking up plans, schemes and products with alarming speed. Somehow the finances would always come together, but always without warning. At the same time, I was going through some personal family trauma that sapped a lot of emotional energy. I was the proverbial headless chicken, with a "Dynamite" fake sense of urgency, second to none.

All of that changed in December 2016. I woke up one morning and just could not get out of bed. It wasn't that I didn't want to—I couldn't. When I eventually did get up in a bit of a haze, I started working but had no energy or focus. This went on for a couple of days and I eventually went to see a doctor because something was broken. I was diagnosed with clinical burn-out, together with the "friendly" twins, anxiety and depression. I was told to do nothing—NOTHING—for at least six weeks. The doctor also suggested anti-depressants for two years. I negotiated him down to six months, like that would make a difference, and fully expected to take a day or two off and then get back on the horse. He was insistent that it wouldn't work like that. Well, it had to, because the bills don't take sick leave.

But, of course, the doctor was right. Just like a car without fuel can't move forward, I was equally stationary. Luckily, I had a friend who had experienced this a few years before and could give me good advice. He told me to be ultra kind to myself. He was also a helping hand and managed to calm me down to be able to follow doctor's orders.

Nothing for six weeks.

I thought I would go mad within a couple of days, but it took three weeks of sleeping when I was tired, eating when I was hungry, watching TV and hardly ever going out of the house, before I felt even an inkling of normal energy levels returning. When I did get back to working, I toned it down completely and only did those tasks that I felt were in line with where I wanted the business to go. Sometimes I didn't have anything to do, and that was okay—I was still recovering. I adopted an approach to do only one thing every day to move the business forward. Eventually, I was on the pills for a year and while my working days were much calmer, I was still making roughly the same amount of turnover. The "Diesel" approach was in no way less successful. The effect of both outcomes of the "Resilience" decision point had been made very clear to me.

The trick is to build in resilience. Others might call it margin. Effectively, it means not to push the envelope all the time, but rather to always leave a little in reserve for when you need it. Continually pushing the envelope may work for the *Top Gun* movie, but it makes for a risky business.

How well do you know yourself? Do you regularly drive yourself and others into hyperactivity? What does the "Resilience" decision mean for you?

YOUR TURN

1. Do you drive yourself and others harder than you should? If so, why?

_____

_____

_____

_____

_____

_____

2. If you have listed reasons above, how true are they really?

_____

_____

_____

_____

3. Do you need to make changes for the sake of your team, family or health?

_____

_____

_____

_____

_____

Importance Scoring (1-10) _____

Discipline: Public or Private?

No matter where you are in your leadership journey, your authority will be challenged. The challenges could be low-key, like a passive-aggressive neglect to fulfill certain requests, or they could be a publicly stated refusal to comply. I am not referring here to healthy debate about solutions where this kind of discussion is warranted. I am referring specifically to someone who is challenging and testing the boundaries of authority. The "Discipline" decision is how to respond to those challenges.

Public. In this scenario, the leader will deal with the challenge in full view of others. This is appropriate when the challenge is also public. It is necessary when the challenge is disruptive to the team. In extreme cases, where leaders deal with *every* perceived challenge publicly, the team members will become insecure and will not speak up in meetings, or even in private, because it could embarrass or otherwise disadvantage them.

Private. In this scenario, the leader will deal with the challenger in private. If the challenge itself was in private, it's entirely appropriate. However, if the challenge was made in public, the "Discipline" decision becomes key. In extreme cases, leaders deal with *all* challenges in private, and often do so because their regard for the challenger's dignity is high. Often, the term used is to "save face". While this seems all good and noble, the team suffers. The leader's ability to lead suffers, and the team perceives fuzzy boundaries where members are unsure of what is acceptable.

Any challenge to authority presents the leader with a unique opportunity. The person who challenges you is not inherently bad, he is simply challenging you for some reason. If it is public, however, everybody is watching to see how you will react and how you will deal with the challenge. They will be keenly interested to see what stands firm, and what they could get away with. You know that such an incident will become the discussion of offices, coffee areas and lift clubs. How you respond to the challenge will let your people know whether they can trust you as their leader. You have a wonderful opportunity here to show the team who you are, and what you stand for.

Sometimes the response needs to be public, and sometimes it's best to deal with it in private. The leader may want more information as to the motivation behind the challenge, and therefore the real story will come out. In this case, the resolution must be made public—with due regard for the team and the challenger. We can, however, make the mistake of seeing the challenge purely as an issue between ourselves and the challenger. We can work hard to resolve the issue privately, but the team is left in the dark, and—in the absence of a properly communicated resolution—they might make the assumption that it was simply let go. This undermines the leader's authority in the eyes of the whole team.

The balance that often needs to be kept when contemplating the "Discipline" decision, is between maximum public value for the team and maximum dignity for the challenger. Each scenario must be weighed on its own merits, such as why the challenger is behaving in a certain way, are there circumstances the leader is unaware of, and so on. On the other hand, feisty public challenges that disrupt the team must be dealt with quickly. A one-size-fits-all approach does not work.

APPLICATION EXAMPLE

I'm a fan of short, daily meetings. They are there to direct the team for the day and give me a good read on what is going on in my area. It's also a time for the team to come together and re-align themselves. Rudi Giuliani[23], New York mayor for eight years and during the 9/11 attacks, managed the city through daily morning meetings. He said, *"The importance of the 'morning meeting' cannot be overstated."* I support that.

I also require that these morning meetings don't waste time and are effective. For that to happen, the meeting has to start on time, every time. A person's time is valuable, and I struggle with the idea that someone can keep a whole team waiting while they attend to "this or that". There will always be a "this or that" to attend to, and if it is allowed, meetings will take 10 minutes or more to get started. It will also invariably be the same people, indicating that it's a behavioral issue, not necessarily a work-related one. If this happens every day, it's almost an hour a week that is lost per person, as well as a source of frustration on the part of the team and a dislike for the meeting. Telling people to "start without me" is equally annoying; the team meeting is for the entire team to know what is going on. When this happens, invariably when the late team member does arrive, a quick summary of what has already been discussed has to be given, again wasting everyone else's time. I seethe when so-called public servants deem it okay to arrive hours late to large meetings and keynotes simply because they are "VIP's", and their time is valuable. And don't get me started on emails and laptops in meetings— but that's for another time.

My foundry team discussed this and came up with a solution. Since a foundry is a hot and smoky place, a cooldrink from the tuck-shop is always welcome. The team suggestion was that since the meeting started at 8am sharp, the person to arrive last, if it is after 8am, must buy a round of cooldrinks for the entire team. Typically, there were about 10 people. The cooldrinks would be available for the team at the following day's 8am meeting, and no, they could not use "buying cooldrinks for the team" as an excuse for being late. They could only be late for the meeting by giving a valid reason ahead of time. The entire team agreed, and we implemented the idea. People were on time for a while, and anyone that was late, including me, had to buy the next round. If I was late often, it got expensive. One morning, one of the managers was the last to arrive, after 8am. Let's call him Joe*. He was a repeat offender who was often a little late. Joe was told by the team that he would be supplying the next day's cooldrinks. He refused. The next day he arrived at the meeting on time, but without the required cooldrinks. He refused to pay out of his own pocket for a work meeting. It was a challenge to the team and the culture that we were trying to foster. It also became a challenge to my authority, since

I had to make the call as to what to do. The "Discipline" decision point loomed.

The most common response would have been to call off the cooldrink penalty idea. I had sympathy for the personal finance side, but it was really within every individual's own control to be at the meeting on time. I was also aware that this was not a life-and-death matter—it was just cooldrinks after all. But it would significantly impact the team culture that I was trying to build. This had been a team decision, and it was being challenged. If the challenge wasn't met head-on, we would slip back to being slack on punctuality. In *Extreme Ownership*, Jocko Willink and Leif Babin[4] rightly state that what you tolerate becomes your standard.

My response to Joe was to acknowledge that the cooldrinks were expensive. I also reminded him that he had it completely within his control to be on time. Finally, I grabbed the opportunity to demonstrate to the entire team what teamwork is. I went out to the tuck-shop and bought the cooldrinks for the team, including Joe, with my own money. In the presence of the team, I explained to Joe that he could be late every day, and I would continue to buy cooldrinks for the whole team, every day. I did not expect him to pay the money back. I said that when one of our team members is unable to fulfill his commitments, the rest of the team steps in to pick up the slack. That is what this

> "Jocko Willink and Leif Babin rightly state that what you tolerate becomes your standard."

foundry team would be all about. I sat down and we went on with the meeting. After the meeting, Joe hounded me to pay back the money for the drinks, but I refused. I told him to rather get organized for the next day so that we did not need to buy cooldrinks, because I didn't have all the money in the world. It had a tremendous effect on the team, who now knew that I was serious about us working as a team, and not just being on time. We all picked up our game accordingly, and a strong team culture—even pride—was formed. Throughout the plant the foundry team was known for effective meetings that started and ended on time, with everybody present. We even managed to get all our training for the year done during these meetings because they were effective. This flowed into all other areas of our teamwork where the team was respected and worked together. Eventually, they amended the penalty system to include other transgressions like answering cellphones during the meeting. They also changed the penalty to cooldrinks on Fridays only and all the weeks' transgressors contributed. And it was done in such a fun way that even visitors to our meetings would insist on contributing if they transgressed.

Is it just cooldrinks? I think not. It's the basic broken-window theory that says if you deal with the little things, you prevent the big things from taking root. But the key was to put the team first and the individual second—without disrespecting the individual. It was done publicly, demonstrating to the team how this teamwork thing actually works. The message was clear to all that each of us was expected to contribute to the team, including myself.

On another occasion, a year or two later, Joe reacted in a negative way in the morning meeting, but this time I had a sense that the private approach would be better. The team had integrated very well, and each manager had his area of responsibility, but every other team member was allowed to question his actions—there were no taboo or no-go areas. Trust was high and it was a team that I was very proud to be part of.

On this particular Monday, one of the team members was questioning Joe on a decision he had made in his area, and he responded in an emotional way, saying the team was welcome to take over if they thought they could do better. Since the team knew that I was big on teamwork, everybody immediately looked at me. I had a sense not to respond and just told the guys to get on with the meeting. When the meeting was over, I asked Joe to come to my office. We discussed what had happened and I also let him know that his response was emotional, and that I was concerned about him. He broke down. As it turned out, he had been under enormous pressure in his department. We all had, it had been a busy time, but his area had borne the brunt of it. His area was also the only area that worked 24/7, so he was always on call. Together with that, he had his fair share of home concerns to take care of as well. He was fried.

I told Joe he should immediately go home and take leave for the rest of the week. At first, he didn't want to, and saw this as punishment. I explained to him that it was neither punishment nor reward. It was necessary for him to survive and be a functioning member of the work team, as well as his home team. One of his shift supervisors was more than able to stand in for him, and he needed to recover. Joe went home, and I explained to the team what had happened. The team stepped up, helping out in his department where they could, and checking in with him to see how he was doing.

The following Monday, when Joe came back to work, our team member was back! The week off was exactly what he needed, and he thanked me for insisting that he go home. A public reaction to his emotional state would have been counter-productive at best, and would have damaged not only Joe, but also the team.

The "Discipline" decision point comes around regularly.

All too often, the little things are not deemed important enough to deal with, and basic discipline fails. Or they are discussed privately, and the team is deprived of a fantastic learning opportunity. Other times, things that should be handled privately, explode publicly, and the team always loses focus. The "Discipline" decision point is not only a reaction to a challenge, but also an opportunity to take the team to a higher level of functioning.

> *"The 'Discipline' decision point is not only a reaction to a challenge, but an opportunity to take the team to a higher level of functioning."*

How do you respond to a challenge? Do you have a method of deciding whether to deal with the challenge publicly or privately? Do you have instances where you were the challenger? What was the response?

YOUR TURN

1. Do you respond to challenges to your authority publicly or privately?

_____

_____

_____

2. Have you considered these to be leadership opportunities? How could you respond to take full advantage?

_____

_____

_____

_____

_____

_____

Importance Scoring (1-10) _____

Positioning: Part of the Team or Apart from the Team?

When you are leading a team, there is a balance between being "one of the guys" and, at the same time, being the respected leader. Depending on the situation that the team faces, either one of the two approaches may be more appropriate. Deciding on a single approach as a standard for all situations may be easier, but probably not as effective as a leader with more flexibility. However, as usual, each of the approaches has extremes that are detrimental to the team's performance and should be avoided.

Part of the team. In this scenario, the leader takes on his fair share of team duties, at the level of a team member. This could happen when another team member is a subject-matter expert and takes the lead for a scenario that requires his expertise. It can also happen when there is simply a lot of work and extra hands are required. It could also be where a leader identifies with his team when an injustice is done to them and he stands with them. There is a memorable turning point in the movie[2], *Glory*, where Colonel Robert Shaw—commander of the first battalion of black soldiers in the civil war—sees his men got paid less than the equivalent white soldiers. The men revolt and tear up their pay sheets, effectively refusing their pay. Shaw draws a pistol, shoots into the air to silence the crowd, and announces, "If you men will take no pay, then none of us will!" and tears up his own pay sheet. From that moment on the men are loyal to their colonel, and the colonel to his men.

Being part of the team can also have negative effects, though. Often, a leader emerges from the ranks of the team and is then put in charge of his old buddies. He was always "one of the team", and still wants that identity. Because of that need, he may be slack on discipline or quality of work. He effectively leaves a leadership vacuum that will make the team uncertain and unfocused. It won't be long before the team becomes inefficient and more involved in petty squabbles than big-picture contribution.

Apart from the team. In this scenario, the leader is not "one of the guys". He is the leader and the team members are the followers. It is important to make this distinction when developing the members of the team. If the leader keeps involving himself in all the details, his voice will naturally carry more weight, and his team members will never learn to make decisions for themselves. A good leader's first priority is to develop the people in his charge, so when a task

> *"A good leader's first priority is to develop the people in his charge."*

comes along that should be handled by the team or specific team members, he must take a step back and allow the team to learn. He must give them the space to succeed or to fail, but always be available to help when appropriate. This means that when the leader is apart from the team, he is still actively involved. Remember also that, in a middle-management setting, the leader of a team is also a team member of the next-level team in the structure, which will require him to be apart from the team at times.

Once again, being apart from the team can have an extreme case. Here, the leader is aloof and removed from his people. He does not identify with them and never becomes part of the team. He simply hands out the tasks and expects them to be done. He never gets involved. This leader may have several reasons for being so disengaged, but none of them will be for the betterment of the team.

In this extreme case, like in the previous example, he leaves a leadership vacuum, and low morale and lack of engagement are sure to follow.

The effective leader makes the "Positioning" decision on a case-by-case basis, depending on what is best for the team, and what results are required. The leader also has an opportunity here to explain, through action, which issues are of importance by ensuring his involvement when those issues arise. His people will then know exactly where they have the freedom to try new things, while other cases require the leader's input.

Making the "Positioning" decision without clear guidelines could result in team members not being sure where they stand on any given day, and where the leader positions himself based on internal and subjective criteria.

APPLICATION EXAMPLE

When I first managed the ABC Manufacturing* foundry, I wanted to be in on everything *and* still part of the team I had evolved from. However, managing a 250-people strong, 24-hour operation, takes more than one person. When I took over the foundry, it was not running that well, since it was still in the throes of having moved to new premises with new technology and historical mindsets. I used to get calls most nights, at all hours. It wasn't long before I became weary of wanting to know everything. I had a few managers reporting to me, and decided we needed to have a few guidelines on when I would be part of the team, and when I would be apart from the team.

The managers all had their areas of control, and I did not need to be informed of everything that happened. I did insist on being called if a crisis started looming or if anyone got injured, no matter how minor. As a backstop, there was a plant-wide nightshift manager who would bring me up to speed on the night's events in a daily phone call while I travelled to the plant in the morning. For all intents and purposes—under normal running conditions—I was apart from the team, although keenly interested in how they were developing.

In any kind of production environment, crises regularly occur. It could be as minor as a machine breakdown, or it could be major, like a systemic material or process flaw that creeps in. In a 24-hour production scenario, the effect is amplified because you lose two to three times more capacity for every day that the crisis is in play. You have to act fast to get the crisis resolved.

When one of the systemic crises occurred, we needed to do round-the-clock experiments to find the cause of the material or process flaw. It could not just be left overnight. In these situations, I would become part of the team. All managers, including myself, were put on shifts to do the experimentation, and I always put myself on night shift first. There were many reasons for this—if you want to know what's really going on in a 24-hour plant, go there at night. Night shifts are also more focused because the daytime meeting routine isn't happening. I tended to get a lot more done during night shifts, and the daytime managers, who were standing in for me, were often given a lot of leeway from the usual meeting routine. In this way, we increased our experimentation capacity by simply not having me there during the day. Most importantly to me, though, it demonstrated to the entire workforce that, as a leader, I was not exempt from the hardships that the team went through during a crisis. It fostered trust and a respectful familiarity with the entire team.

Even when there was no crisis, I sometimes stood in for one of my managers who was ill or on leave. It was not because I didn't trust the people on the floor. It was to stay in touch with what was happening on the floor, and to demonstrate that I was part of the team. Again, this is a fine line, because if I did it too often, I would take away the opportunity for other team members to develop into shop-floor leaders.

How do you approach the "Positioning" decision point? Are you taking on team members' responsibilities more than you should be? Do you jump in when it's necessary?

YOUR TURN

1. How attached are you to being part of the team all the time?

_____

_____

_____

_____

_____

2. What guidelines have you established for your involvement?

Importance Scoring (1-10) _____

Consistency: Dependable Vision or Random Messages?

People like to know where they are going, and what the company is up to. If you've ever been in a situation where ominous rumors are floating around in an organization, and you're not sure of your future, you will know that it's the uncertainty that gets to you. Whether the news is good or bad, you want to have certainty. I've had to talk people out of taking voluntary retrenchment packages, because their sole reason for doing so has been to get rid of uncertainty and not because they wanted to be retrenched. In my coaching work, I've seen uncertain situations literally stop people in their tracks, suspending all action until they worked up the courage to make a decision. I've also seen the same in myself.

Random messages. Leaders must beware of causing uncertainty in their people. Even if the leader feels uncertain, he can communicate this in a way that gives his people comfort. Let's face it, if the leader is always certain, then his job can't be that much of a challenge. Leaders who are too certain are likely going to fall into the "Consistency" trap. Facts change, and suddenly the leader's messages are—without explanation—no longer consistent. People become more uncertain, and the negative rumors take over. More importantly, people lose trust in the leader who contradicts himself too often. It reminds me a bit of radio economists who predict that growth will be strong and wonderful, but the very next day, after a negative incident, they predict the exact opposite without even skipping a beat. Would you entrust your retirement plans to those economists?

Communicating with your people also cannot be a once-off event. If you lead people, you have to keep them informed and you have to gauge where they are and what they are feeling. The leader who occasionally comes down from the mountain with a profound decree, only to disappear up into the clouds again afterwards, has no relationship with the people. And where there is no relationship, there is no trust.

> *"With people, fast is slow, and slow is fast."*

In *The 7 Habits of Highly Effective People*, Stephen Covey states, *"With people, fast is slow, and slow is fast."* This is particularly annoying to driven entrepreneurs who need to be moving at lightspeed. The problem is, they'll always be moving alone, blaming their people for being slow or not of the right caliber.

Dependable vision. If you want success with people, you need to slow down to their pace, then lead them from there to a faster pace, teaching them as you go. In the end, this will get you to where you are all going faster.

Messages must be both constant and very similar in order to be "Dependable". When changes do occur, which they inevitably will, the constant message stream can explain these changes and reasons for them. This builds trust, even if the changes are difficult. In my opinion, this drip-feed messaging is the only way to effectively lead a team—annual team-building sessions are only effective in conjunction with these. By themselves, they are just an expensive, nice day out.

APPLICATION EXAMPLES

In my various roles, especially in 24-hour production areas where there are shifts, I have made a point of personally speaking to the people of each shift, every week for 10 to 15 minutes. While this meant that I had to come in at odd times for the shift changes, it was the most effective way to promote a vision, give active feedback, hear what the issues were, and get the feel of the staff. It isn't just about the message, it's also about perception and emotion that told me where we stood. Included in

"By not taking care with your messaging, you are deciding for random messages and you sabotage your own communication process."

these weekly sessions were short training snippets on safety, leadership, teamwork or disciplinary issues. These were always done in conjunction with the company vision. Initially, the people grumbled about having to go to these meetings, but not too long afterwards some individuals started coming forward after the meetings to ask what additional books they could read, or how they could improve some of the aspects of the manufacturing processes. At that point, if I dared to cancel a meeting for a week, or excuse someone because they had pressing work to do, I would get complaints.

People want to know what is going on.

Whenever you are going to speak to your people, be sure that you know what you have been telling them, what they have been hearing, and that the message is consistent. By not taking care with your messaging, you are deciding for random messages and you sabotage your own communication process! It starts with giving feedback if you have said you would. Even with my weekly meetings, I still managed to fall into the "Consistency" trap a few times, simply by being a bit negligent with my words.

One of my most memorable "Consistency" events happened while negotiating retrenchments at ABC Manufacturing*. As has been stated elsewhere, the unions involved were militant and stubbornly difficult. According to the labor law requirements in South Africa, I had to state reasons and discuss these with the unions over a period of at least 60 days. These 60 days also required at least four facilitated meetings between the unions and the company—facilitated by a commissioner from the Council for Conciliation, Mediation and Arbitration (CCMA). The meetings also included a representative from the employees who were *not* represented by the unions, typically the engineering, finance and design staff. In the meetings, the dire financial state of the auto industry was discussed, and the need for permanent retrenchments was made very clear. Even though the unions fought it, the reasons were sound. Although the news was bad, not taking this step would be disastrous for the continued existence of the company. Outside of the meetings, the atmosphere in the company was subdued and tentative.

Since our retrenchment was part of a longer-term automation project, the consultations took nine months. During this time, as HR director, I was given another task—to replace four of the directors' ageing company cars, including my own. These vehicles were leased, and the leasing costs were borne by the individual directors for the vehicles they chose. It did not impact the company accounts at all. Many of the existing vehicles were becoming unreliable and not worth repairing, and some of the directors travelled over 150 km a day just to work and back.

However, I was concerned about the messaging. On the one hand, we were contemplating retrenchments due to long-term economic pressures, and on the other hand, we would buy new luxury vehicles and park them outside the front door of the building, right next to the entrance turnstiles that everyone used. Despite the fact that the company's financial impact was zero, I knew that the perceptions and rumors would spread like wildfire, saying that we had money for fancy new cars but no money for people's jobs. The costs could not be made explicit because they were part of the directors' salaries, which were confidential. It was a position that could not be defended. At the weekly directors' meeting I suggested that we either delay the vehicle project, or even better, not purchase luxury cars but rather opt for bottom-of-the-range vehicles. This would show the staff that we also felt the negative effects of the economy, and we were on the same team. I was naïve, I guess, but the suggestions were shot down as I was stating them. It made no difference to the company budget, and I was instructed to go ahead. I did warn that this would negatively impact the retrenchment consultations, but that was not seen as a problem. So, I went ahead with the project and went about replacing the four vehicles.

It wasn't long after the first vehicle was on site that the rumors started. In the subsequent retrenchment consultations, the issue did come up, but it was explained how the finances worked and the consultations weren't substantially impacted. However, outside of the formal meetings, I had a number of conversations with employees, and it was clear that the staff had lost a lot of trust in the company leaders. What was most interesting, was that the design and engineering staff—who could best grasp the financial argument—were the most vehement about the fact that this was a slap in the face of the people. While the decision could be financially justified, the perception, motive and messaging were completely misaligned.

Everyone knew it, and I believe we lost a huge opportunity to build trust in those difficult times.

How much time and effort do you put into communication with your people? Do you think before you commit?

YOUR TURN

1. Do you constantly and consistently communicate with your team?

_____

_____

_____

_____

2. Have you found yourself sabotaging your own efforts by not taking due care?

_____

_____

_____

_____

3. What could you do now in order to improve your messages to your people?

_____

_____

_____

_____

Importance Scoring (1-10) _____

Peacemaker: Competition or Collaboration?

At some point, you will be faced with the choice whether to compete or collaborate. I call this the "Peacemaker" decision, because true collaboration is all about making *lasting* peace, while competition does not require peace at all, and in some cases actually disturbs it. It's also not peace *keeping*, which is simply maintaining a superficial peace—not wanting to rock the boat. This decision is all about having the patience and courage to sort out root-cause issues and move forward from there.

Competition. In order for me to win, you must lose. Or at least, I need to win more than you do. It's an easier approach because I only have to look at my interests and can completely ignore yours. It's fast and efficient but can leave the interaction with disgruntled competitors and bad feelings.

Collaboration. In order to win, both parties need to have their requirements fulfilled. Your interests are as important as mine, and we must work together to find a solution that fits us both. It's slow and can be frustrating, but a successful outcome is extremely rewarding. All parties leave the interaction having gained.

> *"On the surface, it would seem that collaborating should always be the way to go, but it isn't effective in all situations."*

On the surface, it would seem that collaborating should always be the way to go, but it isn't effective in all situations. Firstly, it requires that both parties intend to collaborate. If the opposing party just isn't interested, your only choice is to compete. Or to walk away, of course. Secondly, it requires time, and not all decisions will afford that luxury, such as emergency triage decisions. Thirdly, it requires common ground, and there are cases where common ground just can't be found, such as unpopular decisions that cannot be avoided. Finally, it requires that the outcome is important enough to warrant the time and energy, and often the decisions just aren't that big.

Where it does go wrong, though, is when we take a competitive stance on *everything*, whether it's landing a big contract, achieving a bigger sales value than colleagues, or just how we interact with friends at the dinner table. We again have the power to choose, and our choices will determine our effectiveness as a leader.

If you are naturally more competitive, be aware that you may sacrifice relationships in order to win, and consequently everyone loses. If you are naturally more collaborative, be aware that sometimes you will still be launching from the starting blocks while someone else has already finished the work. Which approach to follow is entirely dependent on the particular situation at hand—which is why this is classified as a "Behavioral" decision point.

APPLICATION EXAMPLES

The retrenchment negotiations, which I referred to in the "Freedom" decision point, are an example of where I was forced to work in a competitive mode by an adversary who refused to collaborate. However, the decisions and the outcome were extremely important, and a collaborative style would have been much more effective. When the agreements were eventually signed, it was done with a resignation to the fact by the union, a feeling of defeat for them, and a hollow victory for the company. All the issues that were raised in the consultations would inevitably resurface down the line, and the relationship between the company and the employees was damaged. The agreement itself had not caused the animosity, the competition approach had. Had the union been open to—and allowed—a collaborative approach, the agreement would have been welcomed. Unions do not need to be competitive in order to be effective. I have been party to discussions with other unions where the discussions were at a mature and collaborative level, with much better outcomes in terms of employer-employee relationships.

In sales, it should be obvious that a collaborative approach is best with customers. However, many salespeople seem to approach their customers as a competition—a challenge to conquer. Think of some of the pushy telemarketers you've dealt with—definitely a competition to see who will win.

In my time at consulting firm, triVector, we went out of our way to collaborate with our clients. Obviously we also had our share of difficult projects, but whereas some of the other companies were protecting IP (intellectual property) and putting in contractual clauses for extra payments, we took the approach of sharing everything, as long as it was ours to share. Our approach was to fully put the clients' interests first, and add value where we could. We did not pad our offering unnecessarily in order to maximize our income. We sold what we believed was required. This led to some long-standing relationships with clients, which even turned into friendships. Importantly for business, it meant that both parties were learning from each other, because as we shared with our clients, so did our clients share with us. Trust became high, and engagements grew from being a resource on a project to becoming a mentor to client personnel and an advisor to the project owners. The endorsement for the pure collaboration approach came from one of our clients when they simply stated that it was always easy and a pleasure to work with us, as opposed to another company where the client had to jump through hoops to get good service. Note that both consulting companies were equally competent.

How competitive are you? How often do you consider using a collaborative approach? Would your team or your colleagues describe you as a "Peacemaker"? What do you need to do to enhance this skill?

YOUR TURN

1. What is your natural style? Competition or collaboration?

_____

_____

2. What challenges are you facing where a collaborative approach would be most effective?

_____

_____

_____

_____

_____

_____

3. How will you go about addressing that challenge?

_____

_____

_____

_____

_____

_____

_____

_____

_____

Importance Scoring (1-10) _____

EPILOGUE — THE COMPLETED DECISION POINT HOUSE

A good story will tell you something about yourself. All the points and stories you've read up to this point have defined what my "Decision Point House" looks like. There are many more instances and stories, but they don't define a new decision point, only a confirmation of earlier ones. I'm not sure about you, but I find some satisfaction in boiling down all this data into a simple, one-page picture that captures the essence of what I value when making decisions.

Taking a step back from my "Decision Point House" picture and just observing what I see there, tells me something about myself. I can remember how the decision points that came my way constructed this house, and I have a fair idea how I will react to certain decision points that will come my way in the future. There probably will be new ones that I haven't encountered yet. I can also uncomfortably recognize those decision points where I may be vulnerable. These are the ones that I struggle to make quickly, or where I go with the rest of the crowd without thinking. It's up to me to further define my "Decision Point House" as I go along.

Whenever I read a book or watch a movie, I'm conscious of my emotions when it finishes. Does it leave me fulfilled and worth devoting my time to? Or does it leave me dissatisfied, unsure of its ending, or in some cases, a total waste of the time I've put in? I'm hoping that, at this point, you feel like the story hasn't ended yet, that there is still something missing. You may vehemently disagree with some of my experiences and actions, and want to change some of the details. You may consider some naïve and idealistic. You may be wondering how all this applies to you, or what a "Decision Point House" would look like if your experiences were used to build it.

If that is what you are thinking, then welcome to the last part of this book...

PART C: BUILD YOUR OWN HOUSE

In order to make this book more worthwhile and relevant, you now get to build your own house. This is not a psychometric test, nor is it backed up by cupboards full of research. This is you, evaluating yourself in a simple way to gain some insight into the decisions you make, what you value, and how important those values are to you. The only right answer is the answer that most closely resembles you at this point in time.

A blank "Decision Point House" picture is provided on page 208. The instructions below will culminate in a house that has been completely filled in.

The instructions are simple, and all you need is a pen and some time to think.

1. If you have not done so already, then go through the "References" questions that were asked in Part A, at the end of each section (the ones that start with "Your Turn"), and interrogate your own thoughts and beliefs. You may also identify some additional topics and may choose to completely discard some of mine. Your choice. The important part is to identify the thoughts and

beliefs you hold and make an assessment of how powerful they are in your life.

2. From this exercise you may identify false beliefs that need changing. List them and think of one or two steps you could take to replace them with more helpful beliefs.

3. Transfer your identified "Reference" topics to the blank house's "References" blocks.

4. If you have not already done so, go through the questions at the end of every "Decision Point" section.

5. Decide for each of the decision points which one of the outcomes best describes your thinking.

6. Score each decision point independently on a 10-point score, where 1 means it is of no importance to you, while 10 means it absolutely defines you.

7. Transfer your scores and outcomes into the summary table. By looking at the summarized table, you can consider which of these decision points are "Foundational", "Character" or "Behavioral". It does not necessarily follow that your highest scores are the foundational ones, but the scores do help you prioritize within the categories. The summary table also has some blank lines for your additional decision points, and you are welcome to cross out the ones you feel don't feature in your life. I have placed a section of my summary table on the next page as an example:

No.	Name	Decision Point Outcome	Score	Type
1	Impact: Play to Win or Play Not to Lose?	Absolutely Play to Win. Or fail trying.	10	F
10	Freedom: Manipulate or Emancipate?	Emancipate for sure, but here and there I may end up manipulating. I absolutely don't enjoy being manipulated!	9	C
21	Consistency: Dependable Vision or Random Messages?	I'll always try and keep the vision consistent, but circumstances sometimes change and may have to double-back.	9	B

8. Transfer your foundational, character and behavioral decision points to the blank "Decision Point House" provided.

You now have a "Decision Point House" that describes you. However, the importance of this exercise is not to construct the house, it is to go through the thinking process that percolates out the information to construct your house. This is where you will have gained insight into yourself.

Your Decision Point House

If you have identified new decision points for yourself, note them down in the spaces below.

1. New   Decision   Point:

_____

_____

_____

_____

_____

_____

How might your frame of reference affect this decision point?

_____

_____

_____

_____

_____

Importance Scoring (1-10) _____

2. New   Decision   Point:

_____

_____

_____

_____

_____

_____

_____

_____

How might your frame of reference affect this decision point?

_____

_____

_____

_____

Importance Scoring (1-10) _____

3. New   Decision   Point:

_____

_____

_____

_____

_____

_____

How might your frame of reference affect this decision point?

_____

_____

Importance Scoring (1-10) _____

Transfer your scores to the summary table below, along with the outcome for each decision point that describes you best. You can then evaluate your decision points and decide whether they are foundational, character or behavioral decision points. Note that the scores don't necessarily indicate what category they belong in. Enter the type (F, C or D) into the right-hand column.

No.	Name	Decision Point Outcome	Score	Type
1	Impact: Play to Win or Play Not to Lose?			
2	Respect: All or Just Some?			
3	Emphasis: To Serve or To Be Served?			
4	Priority: People First or Finance First?			
5	Perspective: Eternal or Earthly?			

No.	Name	Decision Point Outcome	Score	Type
6	Contribution: Serving Down or Serving Up?			
7	Model: Example or Excuse?			
8	Teachability: Tell You or Teach Me?			
9	Authenticity: Open Book or Guarded Vault?			
10	Freedom: Manipulate or Emancipate?			
11	Ego: Conviction or Stubbornness?			
12	Pressure: Popular or Principle?			
13	Criticism: Energizing or Discouraging?			

No.	Name	Decision Point Outcome	Score	Type
14	Intentionality: Growth or Stagnation?			
15	Source: Intuition or Information?			
16	Diligence: Wing It or Work At It?			
17	Commitment: Promise or Possibility?			
18	Resilience: Diesel or Dynamite?			
19	Discipline: Public or Private?			
20	Positioning: Part of the Team or Apart from the Team?			
21	Consistency: Dependable Vision or			

No.	Name	Decision Point Outcome	Score	Type
	Random Messages?			
22	Peacemaker: Competition or Collaboration?			
23				
24				
25				
26				
27				
28				

No.	Name	Decision Point Outcome	Score	Type
29				
30				

Instructions

- Transfer your identified reference topics to the blank house's "References" blocks on the next page.

- Transfer your "Foundational" decision points to the blank house's foundation blocks.

- Transfer your "Character" decision points to the blank house's wall blocks.

- Transfer your "Behavioral" decision points to the blank roof tile blocks.

- Take a few steps back to observe your house.

- What four insights immediately come to mind?

- Write down your insights regarding your "References".

- Write down your insights regarding your "Foundational" decision points.

- Write down your insights regarding your "Character" decision points.

- Write down your insights regarding your "Behavioral" decision points.

- Add some general thoughts if you want to.

Blank Decision Point House

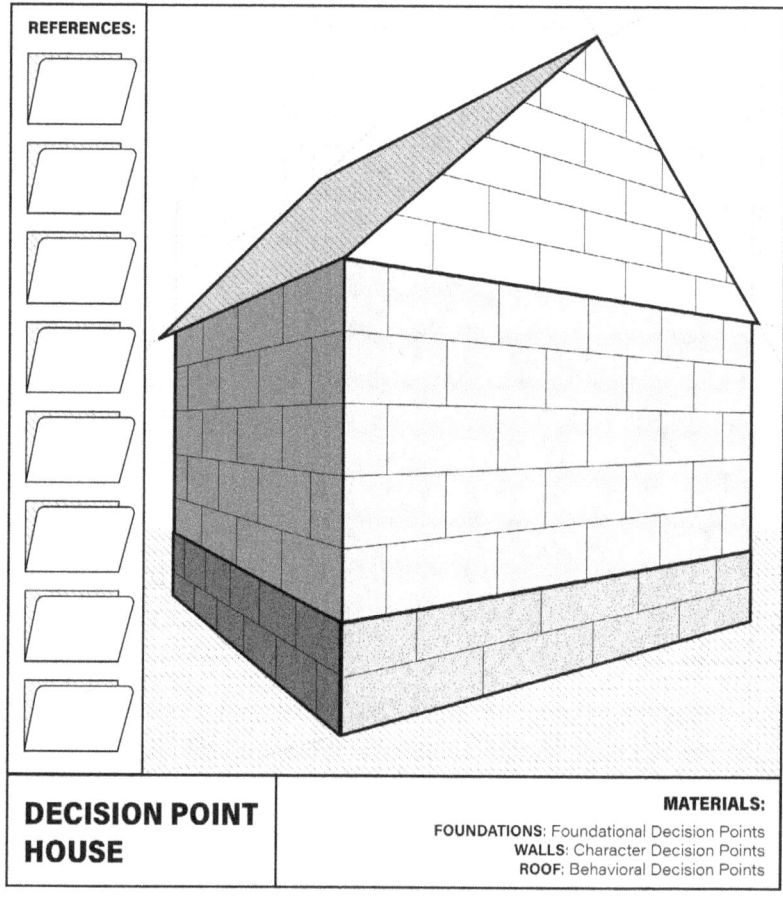

FIRST INSIGHT – REFERENCES

_____

_____

_____

_____

_____

_____

_____

_____

_____

_____

_____

_____

_____

_____

_____

_____

_____

_____

_____

_____

_____

_____

_____

_____

SECOND INSIGHT – FOUNDATIONAL

Third Insight – Character

_____

_____

_____

_____

_____

_____

_____

_____

_____

_____

_____

_____

_____

_____

_____

_____

_____

_____

_____

_____

_____

_____

_____

_____

_____

_____

_____

_____

FOURTH INSIGHT – BEHAVIORAL

GENERAL THOUGHTS

WHAT HAPPENS NOW?

"Tell me and I forget, teach me and I may remember,
involve me and I learn."   –   Benjamin
Franklin

"In learning you will teach, and in teaching you will
learn."   –   Phil
Collins

I trust that going through this material has revealed
much to you. You have grown, which means that you
are in a position to grow others—your team, your family,
your social circles—through your example and in some
cases even formal teaching. The
most effective way of remembering
anything, and for it to really embed
itself in your DNA, is to teach it to
others.

"The most effective
way of remembering
anything, and for it to
really embed itself in
your DNA, is to teach
it to others."

Another way of internalizing
your insights effectively is to talk
about them with others. I would
love to hear your feedback.

Feel free to contact me at
dieter@dieterjansengroup.com. Rest assured I will not

share your stories unless I have your prior permission to do so.

Finally, if you would like your team to build their "Decision Point House", feel free to contact me for pointers and advice on how to do it best. I will not be keeping secrets that only I am able to facilitate—that's not what this book is about.

Keep learning, keep teaching, keep growing.

LIST OF REFERENCES

1. Jim Collins, *Good to Great*, Random House, 2001.

2. *Glory*, Director Edward Zwick, 1989.

3. *Band of Brothers*, Director Steven Spielberg, 2001.

4. Jocko Willink and Leif Babin, *Extreme Ownership*, St. Martin's, 2015.

5. James Allen, *As a Man Thinketh*, Dover, 2007 (original publication 1921).

6. Maxwell Maltz, *The New Psycho-Cybernetics*, Penguin, 2001.

7. John C Maxwell, *The 21 Irrefutable Laws of Leadership*, Thomas Nelson, 2007.

8. Malcolm Gladwell, *Outliers*, Hachette Audio, 2008. Audiobook.

9. John C Maxwell, *There's No Such Thing as "Business" Ethics*, Center Street, 2003.

10. Weldon Long, *The Power of Consistency*, Wiley, 2013.

11. Jon S Rennie, *I have the Watch*, Deck & Conn, 2019. Audiobook.

12. Arbinger Institute, *Leadership and Self-deception*, Audible, 2000. Audiobook.

13. Bob Burg and John David Mann, *The Go-Giver*, Penguin, 2007.

14. The Bible, *New King James Version* (NKJV), Thomas Nelson, 1982.

15. The Bible, *New International Version* (NIV), Zondervan, 1984.

16. Simon Sinek, *Live2Lead 2016 Keynote*, 2016.

17. John C Maxwell, *Leadership Gold*, Thomas Nelson, 2008.

18. Neil Rackham, *SPIN Selling*, McGraw-Hill, 1988.

19. Shannon Thomas, *Healing from Hidden Abuse*, MAST, 2016.

20. *Invictus*, Director Clint Eastwood, 2009.

21. Colin Powell, *It worked for Me: In Life and Leadership*, Harper Audio, 2012. Audiobook.

22. Paul C. Donders, *Resilience*, De Barbaar, 2015.

23. Rudi Giuliani, *Leadership*, Little, Brown, 2002.

24. Stephen R Covey, *The 7 Habits of Highly Effective People*, Simon & Schuster, 1989.

www.ingramcontent.com/pod-product-compliance
Lightning Source LLC
Chambersburg PA
CBHW070532220526
45467CB00003B/933